Canadian Manufacturing

Volume II

The Canadian Institute for Economic Policy has been established to engage in public discussion of fiscal, industrial and other related public policies designed to strengthen Canada in a rapidly changing international environment.

The Institute fulfills this mandate by sponsoring and undertaking studies pertaining to the economy of Canada and disseminating such studies. Its intention is to contribute in an innovative way to the development of public policy in Canada.

Canadian Institute for Economic Policy
Suite 409, 350 Sparks St., Ottawa K1R 7S8

Canadian Manufacturing

A Study in Productivity and Technological Change

Volume II
Industry Studies 1946-1977

Uri Zohar

Canadian Institute for Economic Policy

The opinions expressed in this study are those of the author alone and are not intended to represent those of any organization with which he may be associated.

ISBN 0-88862-613-4 paper
ISBN 0-88862-614-2 cloth

6 5 4 3 2 1   82 83 84 85 86 87

Canadian Cataloguing in Publication Data
Zohar, Uri, 1931-
    Canadian manufacturing: a study in productivity and technological change

Contents: v. 1. Sector performance and industrial strategy — v. 2. Industry studies 1946-1977.
ISBN 0-88862-527-8 (v. 1 bound). — ISBN 0-88862-526-X (v. 1 pbk.). — ISBN 0-88862-614-2 (v. 2 bound). — ISBN 0-88862-613-4 (v. 2 pbk.)

1. Canada — Industries. 2. Industrial productivity — Canada. 3. Canada — Economic policy — 1945-1971.* 4. Canada — Economic policy — 1971-   * I. Canadian Institute for Economic Policy. II. Title.

V.2

HC115.Z64 *1982* 338.0971   C82-095391-5

61,493

Additional copies of this book may be purchased from:

James Lorimer & Company, Publishers
Egerton Ryerson Memorial Building
35 Britain Street
Toronto Ontario, M5A 1R7

Printed and bound in Canada

Contents

Tables

Figures

xviii

Acknowledgements

Detailed industry studies are possible only with the help and co-operation of many people. In the course of this project I have gained a great deal of insight from a wide range of people and trade organizations. I would like to express my appreciation to the Shoe Manufacturers Association and the Electric and Electronic Manufacturing Association of Canada and their respective presidents, Jean-Guy Maheu and David E. P. Armour, for providing me with valuable feedback on my work. Several new ideas were generated through a number of discussions with highly knowledgeable persons of the Department of Industry, Trade and Commerce in Ottawa, following a formal presentation of my findings. Just to mention a few, Messrs. Pierre Marceau, Director-General, Textile and Consumer Products Branch; James A. Adams and R. H. Saver of the Research and Planning Group; Jean-Paul Roy, Chief, Leather and Footwear Division; Jerome A. Doyle, Chief, Furniture and Leisure Products; and M. Chapleau, Director, Policy Issues. My research assistants, Karl Feiler and George Kerr have performed continuously beyond their regular duties.

The Canadian Institute for Economic Policy has been most generous with its provision of an editorial assistant and other services. Specifically, Dr. Roger Voyer and Professor Abraham Rotstein have provided support and patience beyond description to make this project possible. The two referees selected by the Institute provided me with valuable comments.

Mrs. Michelle Srebrolow's willingness to bear with me through several revisions, retyping and corrections to the manuscript is greatly valued.

Needless to say, responsibility for any errors lies exclusively with me.

Introduction

1

This volume is the second of two that comprise my study of the economic performance of the Canadian manufacturing sector from 1946 until 1977. Initially I was interested in the problem of declining productivity growth in recent years which seemed to be especially severe in manufacturing industries. My approach to the problem was to undertake an econometric analysis of the nineteen industries at the two-digit level of the Statistics Canada Standard Industrial Classification, using four different production functions. From the data generated I was able to make some judgments about the performance of several variables in each industry. These conclusions will be especially useful for policy-makers concerned with the development of macroeconomic policy as well as those in government and industry whose decisions are directed more specifically towards sectoral or particular industries.

Volume I, *Sector Performance and Industrial Strategy*, examines the recent literature on the problem of slowing productivity growth in Canada and the United States. It provides a careful introduction to the four production functions used in the analysis — the Cobb-Douglas (CD), constant elasticity of substitution (CES), the variable elasticity of substitution (VES), and the Translog — describing their usefulness as well as their limitations. That volume then examines the average performance of several important variables in the sector over time, drawing on data from Statistics Canada. More important, the sectoral averages are then disaggregated by industry group and by several subperiods to show us what happened at the industry level at different times, and especially in the period after the 1973 energy crisis.

From this exercise I drew at least two critical conclusions. First, the average performance indicators for the manufacturing sector mask quite disparate behaviour from industry to industry and from period to period. Second, although the information about industry performance levels is useful, what is more critical for policy-makers is the rate of change in the variables because, although the level of performance of an industry at any time may seem acceptable, in fact the rate of growth may be increasing unacceptably or indeed may even be declining. Policies would thus likely need to be adjusted to counter falling growth rates.

My major recommendation stems from these findings. Since industries in the manufacturing sector may be growing or for that matter experiencing a slowdown at different times, macroeconomic policy is unlikely to be beneficial to all of them at once. Thus decision-makers must be clear what it is they are trying to accomplish. The mix of policies ultimately adopted must reflect choices about objectives such as growth, stimulation, employment, and regional development. Choosing objectives in our multidimensional society is never an easy task. Nevertheless, once a decision is made about economic and social goals, a coherent strategy can be developed for the manufacturing sector to achieve such aims and accommodate the idiosyncrasies of our manufacturing industries. Volume I concludes by suggesting one way of approaching the formulation of industrial policy to encourage development and productivity growth in the sector.

This volume contains the detailed data on the variables examined for each of the nineteen industries, finishing with a general summary of the sector's performance. It draws on the methodology established in Volume I, and readers are referred there for an understanding of the production functions analysis. This volume can, however, be read without reference to the companion volume. Nevertheless, a brief explanation of some of the concepts and their significance may be useful.

A Guide to the Concepts

Discussion of the concepts follows the order in which the variables appear in the analysis of each industry: capacity utilization, labour productivity, capital intensity, real earnings, technological change, and economies of scale.

The purpose of measuring or estimating indices of capacity utilization is to achieve a quantitative assessment of the potential output and thus the income forgone by the firm or the industry because it did not fully utilize its production resources. The capacity utilization level (or index) therefore represents a degree of resource allocation. Generally, full capacity operation indicates high productivity or efficient allocation of the factors of production. A difficulty arises when we try to identify the forces that cause a gap between the potential and actual output of the industry. For example, is the gap a result of supply-side factors of production or of some market demand fluctuations? To answer such questions satisfactorily, an in-depth study of an industry and its markets must be conducted. Here we do not expect to pinpoint all the causes and their consequences; rather, we can identify supply-side factors through our productivity analysis.

The next set of variables, the structural variables of labour productivity, capital intensity, real earnings, and economies of scale, should be consistent with or bear some relationship to each other. Some economists contend that the prime cause of the productivity slowdown in North America has been the declining rate of growth in capital intensity or the net capital stock per man-hour. This is related to a neglected issue in current economic literature; that is, the explicit measurement of the impact of new capital, through new technology, on labour efficiency. Another neglected area in productivity analyses is the empirical relationship between labour productivity and real earnings per hour.

In economic theory a desirable state is reached when labour receives its marginal product in real wages. Following this theory, if labour receives far below its marginal product, some sort of labour exploitation must exist. Conversely, if labour receives in wages more than it actually produces, firms incur losses; or, if their products are necessities and highly price inelastic, the excess payment to labour is transferred to the consumer in the form of higher prices, which in turn create inflationary pressures. Ideally an increase in capital intensity should lead to an increase in labour productivity; an increase in real earnings should be guided by an increase in productivity; and a rise in economies of scale should contribute to a more than proportionate increase in output.

I examined these relationships with three policy questions in mind. First, is it empirically true that the prime factor for increased labour productivity is an increase in capital intensity? Second, if an industry's level of productivity is sensitive to the introduction of new technology embodied in new capital stock, what is the extent of its response to technological improvements? If it is a highly responsive industry, perhaps it would be worthwhile for the government to help the industry intensify its capital. If the industry does not respond to increased capital by increasing its productivity, perhaps no incentives from the government should be directed to it. Third, does the industry manage to establish a balanced relationship with its labour force, such that

3

labour is not paid an earnings rate that exceeds its marginal productivity? As expected, the answers varied from industry to industry.

By studying the results of the estimations and calculations of variables in the production functions and other relations, the relationships among labour and capital productivity, capital intensity, and real earnings are drawn to verify the existence of connections between, say, capital intensity and labour productivity as production theory implies. I further examine the consistency between theoretical propositions that labour should receive its marginal product in terms of real earnings (the usual first order conditions for all production functions), and several other propositions. The relation between capital intensity and labour productivity is important, because there is increasing agreement among economists lately that the prime cause for the productivity slowdown in North America is the decline in the rate of growth in capital intensity. It is also important because governments must often grant or loan large sums to industries in order to enhance their productivity performance, and this more often than not increases their debts, adds inflationary pressures to the economy, and does not help to improve productivity. In order to provide a complete picture of an industry's productivity performance I examine average levels and then annual rates of growth.

A more specific measure derived from the VES production function assesses the impact of technology on labour efficiency. The value of the variable (m) represents the elasticity of the response to a change in technology. When m equals zero, labour efficiency does not depend on technology; that is, capital is not complementary to labour efficiency. When m is greater than one, capital is complementary to labour efficiency, and technology is more productive than in the case where m is less than one. Complementing this measure is the technological progress function, g, which signals that technology in an industry is basically labour-saving or capital-using when its value is less than one.

The ease with which factors of production can be substituted for one another within a given technology without reducing total production is also estimated through the VES production function. The variable σ represents the degree of such ease, defined as "elasticity of substitution." When σ assumes values greater than one, the factors of production are similar in terms of production technology and hence can be relatively easily substituted for one another. When the values are less than one, factors are dissimilar and substitution is therefore relatively difficult without reducing total production. It stands to

4

reason, therefore, that in a capital-intensive technology, labour cannot easily be substituted for capital without reducing total output. This substitutability is often a high priority policy matter, because if factors of production are easily substituted, then the expansion of an industry could reduce unemployment. If this attribute is measured properly and governments are aware of potential substitutability, they could ease local unemployment situations by inducing the industry to expand.

Another issue analysed for each industry is the impact of economies of scale on productivity. Economists often claim that one of the main sources of high cost and low productivity in Canadian manufacturing has been the smallness of our markets, the short production runs, and thus the inability of industries to attain economies of scale. On a priori grounds, such an argument could be challenged because there is adequate evidence that even smaller economies than the Canadian one have developed highly productive and internationally competitive industries utilizing high quality labour and capital. Indeed, most Canadian industries experienced significant levels of economies of scale, though the impact on productivity varied from industry to industry. The degree of economies of scale is indicated in the data by the size of the scale figure. For example, a figure of 1.38 signifies that an increase in input by a factor of 1 raised scale economies by 1.38. Numbers close to one suggest a minimal effect.

The Productivity Problem

Clearly, rates of growth in total productivity vary for a number of reasons, which may be internal or external to the industry, or some combination of both. Internally, they could be the result of changes either in labour or capital productivity. They could be caused by a significant change in labour quality or changes in capital quality and intensity. Changes as a result of external influences could be caused by variations in the relative price of inputs as a result of, for example, tariff imposition on imported capital goods, world energy price increases, an ''out-of line'' increase in the rate of real earnings, and so forth. My detailed study of the Canadian manufacturing sector has led me to the conclusion that the less than optimal quality of capital is one of the most pervasive problems in the Canadian economy. The empirical evidence in the following chapters supports this view.

Food and Beverage Products Industries

2

This is the largest industry group in the sector, containing 4,521 establishments and contributing 14 per cent to its value added output. It is also a relatively high energy content industry.

Capacity Utilization

Figure 2-1 shows the potential capacity output of this industry group, had it used the total resources at its direct command, and the actual value added output. The difference between these two indicates the unutilized capacity through time. Capacity utilization in the industry was 100 per cent in 1946, dropped gradually to 80.7 per cent in 1963, increased to 82.6 per cent in 1967, and decreased to 72.6 per cent in 1977 (see Volume I, Table 3-1), following the classic V-shaped pattern for the thirty-two years. Compared with the average performance in the manufacturing sector in the 1946-60 period, when capacity utilization increased by a compounded annual rate of 0.02 per cent, the annual rate in this industry decreased by 1.36 per cent. In the 1960s the same inverse relation between the two prevailed; the manufacturing sector increased its capacity utilization by 1.15 per cent annually, while that in the food and beverage products industry decreased by 0.45 per cent per year. In the 1970-77 period, capacity utilization decreased in the manufacturing sector by 0.34 per cent per year, while the annual decrease in utilization in this industry was 1.18 per cent per year. However, after the post-energy crisis period of 1973-77, the sector's capacity utilization showed an annual decrease of 2.57 per cent, while the industry's annual rate of decrease was 1.59 per cent. It is clear from these results that, although the industry is a relatively high energy user, the energy crisis had no significant impact on the food industry's capacity utilization. The rate of decrease in utilization during 1946-60 was similar to that in 1973-77 and higher than the annual rate of decrease from 1970 to 1977. This finding raises a question about the impact of the energy crisis on the food industry, the excuse for rising prices that is so often advanced.

FIGURE 2-1
CAPACITY UTILIZATION, FOOD AND BEVERAGE PRODUCTS INDUSTRIES
(in 1971 constant dollars)

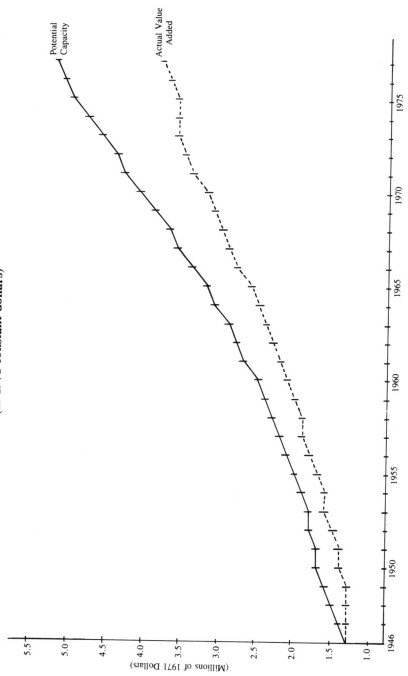

Source: Volume I, Table 3-1 (for all chapters).

7

Labour Productivity, Capital Intensity, Real Earnings, and Economies of Scale

Figure 2-2 shows the rate of change of labour productivity, capital intensity, and real earnings per man-hour. Table 2-1 displays the average performance for the industry in comparison with the sectoral average in these same three categories. The table shows that average annual labour productivity was consistently above the sector's average by a range of 12 to 24 per cent. In fact, average annual productivity rose continuously from the early 1950s. Real earnings and capital intensity per hour exhibited somewhat different growth trends during the last two periods. Average real earnings per hour increased by about one dollar per period in each of the three decades. However, while labour productivity was above the sectoral average throughout the whole period, real earnings were below the sectoral average until 1973. During the 1973-77 subperiod, real earnings in the food and beverage industry exceeded the sectoral average by 3 per cent per annum. Average capital intensity increased steadily from 1946 to 1970, though it remained somewhat below the sector average. Average annual capital intensity increased more significantly between 1970 and 1977, with the 1973-77 subperiod experiencing the highest capital intensity in thirty-two years.

FIGURE 2-2
RATES OF CHANGE IN LABOUR PRODUCTIVITY, CAPITAL INTENSITY, REAL EARNINGS AND ECONOMICS OF SCALE, FOOD AND BEVERAGES PRODUCTS INDUSTRIES
(in 1971 constant dollars)

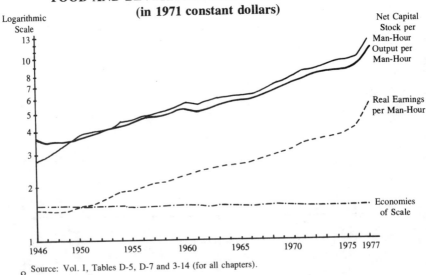

Source: Vol. I, Tables D-5, D-7 and 3-14 (for all chapters).

8

TABLE 2-1

**AVERAGE ANNUAL PERFORMANCE OF LABOUR PRODUCTIVITY,
CAPITAL INTENSITY, AND REAL EARNINGS,
FOOD AND BEVERAGE PRODUCTS INDUSTRIES**

	Food and Beverage	Total Manu.	Industry/ Sector
	(1971 $/hour)		(%)
Labour Productivity			
1946-77	5.55	4.93	112.58
1946-60	4.08	3.50	116.57
1960-70	6.67	5.34	124.91
1970-77	8.33	7.43	112.11
1973-77	8.82	7.79	113.22
Capital Intensity			
1946-77	5.95	5.58	106.63
1946-60	4.16	4.47	93.06
1960-70	6.33	6.67	94.90
1970-77	9.29	9.11	101.98
1973-77	9.95	9.53	104.41
Real Earnings			
1946-77	2.51	2.75	91.27
1946-60	1.77	2.07	85.51
1960-70	2.65	2.96	89.53
1970-77	3.77	3.79	99.47
1973-77	4.05	3.92	103.32

From a policy point of view and the observation of structural change, it is more useful to examine the annual compounded rates of change in these categories, or changes on the margin. Table 2-2 shows that the range of change in labour productivity decreased from 4.99 per cent per year in the 1946-60 period to 2.91 per cent in the 1960-70 period. During the same periods the annual rate of change in real earnings increased from 3.17 during 1946-60 to 3.31 per cent during 1960-70. In the 1970-77 period the significant increase in labour productivity exceeded the sector average by 76 per cent per year. A corresponding rate of annual increases occurred in real earnings and capital intensity. In hourly real earnings the industry progressed from 12 per cent above the sector average in the 1960s to over three times the sector average in the 1970s, while the increase in labour productivity, compared with that in the sector for these subperiods, was much smaller.

Observing whether these rates of increase (included in capital intensity) occurred primarily prior to 1973 or between 1973 and 1977, Table 2-2 and Figure 2-2 show that the rate of change in labour productivity increased from 4.71 per cent per year in the 1970-73 subperiod to an astounding 7.37 per cent per year since 1973, or three times the increase in the sector. Real earnings sustained an annual rate of increase of 4.19 per cent between 1970 and 1973 and 9.83 per cent since 1973, or almost five times the sectoral rate of increase. It is therefore clear that the energy crisis had no bearing on labour productivity and real earnings in this industry.

The trend of capital intensity was somewhat different in the post-energy crisis era. The rate of change in capital intensity declined

TABLE 2-2

COMPOUNDED ANNUAL RATES OF CHANGE IN LABOUR
PRODUCTIVITY, CAPITAL INTENSITY, AND REAL EARNINGS,
FOOD AND BEVERAGE PRODUCTS INDUSTRIES

(% in 1971 constant dollars)

	Food and Beverage	Total Manu.	Industry/ Sector
Labour Productivity			
1946-77	3.83	3.70	103.51
1946-60	4.99	3.82	130.63
1960-70	2.91	3.64	79.95
1970-77	6.22	3.53	176.20
1970-73	4.71	5.04	93.45
1973-77	7.37	2.41	305.81
Capital Intensity			
1946-77	4.99	3.83	130.29
1946-60	5.35	4.99	107.21
1960-70	3.29	2.34	140.60
1970-77	6.73	3.66	183.88
1970-73	8.37	1.90	404.5
1973-77	4.59	5.01	91.07
Real Earnings			
1946-77	4.02	2.85	141.05
1946-60	3.17	3.27	96.94
1960-70	3.31	2.94	112.59
1970-77	7.37	2.31	319.05
1970-73	4.19	2.72	154.04
1973-77	9.83	2.01	489.05

significantly after 1973, following the strong increase in the 1970-73 period. This variable for the industry fell below the sector average in 1973 for the first time since 1946.

Table 2-3 outlines the structural relationships in this industry. Included are data on average productivity and real earnings in order to demonstrate that averages over the whole period are grossly misleading for policy purposes. For example, on average it appears that in this industry labour productivity was double the real earnings paid to labour; in other words, labour received only half of its contribution to productivity. But it is far more useful to ask whether changes in the rate of productivity were followed by changes in the real earnings rate. The answer is that in the 1946-60 period the rate of productivity growth was 57 per cent greater than the rate of growth in real earnings. In the last seventeen years of data, the rate of increase in real earnings outstripped the rate of growth in productivity by a factor of 1.13 to 1.19. During the 1970-73 subperiod, however, labour received in real

TABLE 2-3

RATIO OF LABOUR PRODUCTIVITY/EARNINGS, OUTPUT/CAPITAL, AND TECHNOLOGICAL CHANGE, FOOD AND BEVERAGE PRODUCTS INDUSTRIES

(in 1971 constant dollars)

	1946-77	1946-60	1960-70	1970-77	1970-73	1973-77
	AVERAGE LABOUR PRODUCTIVITY/AVERAGE REAL EARNINGS					
Total manufacturing	1.79	1.69	1.80	1.96		1.99
Food and Beverage	2.21	2.31	1.77	2.21		2.18
	COMPOUNDED RATES OF CHANGE IN LABOUR PRODUCTIVITY/REAL EARNINGS					
Total manufacturing	1.30	1.17	1.24	1.53	1.85	1.20
Food and Beverage	0.95	1.57	0.88	0.84	1.12	0.75
	AVERAGE OUTPUT/AVERAGE CAPITAL					
Total manufacturing	0.81	0.80	0.81	0.82	0.83	0.82
Food and Beverage	0.92	1.00	0.92	0.90	0.92	0.89
	COMPOUNDED RATES OF CHANGE IN OUTPUT/CAPITAL					
Total manufacturing	−0.14	−1.14	1.30	−0.16	2.95	−2.43
Food and Beverage	−1.27	−2.55	0.00	−0.46	0.00	−0.91
	COMPOUNDED RATES OF CHANGE IN TECHNOLOGY (%)					
	1946-77	1960-70	1970-77			
Total manufacturing	0.271	0.259	0.361			
Food and Beverage	- 0.062	−0.132	0.159			

wages only 0.89 of the increase in productivity, while in the 1973-77 subperiod the rate of growth in earnings outstripped the rate of growth in labour productivity by 33.3 per cent. The implication is that if the products of this industry are relatively price inelastic — and food products are viewed as a necessity — these excess payments to labour were by and large transferred to the consumer. This provides at least a partial explanation of why the price of food rose at a faster rate than the average consumer price index. Consumers have had to pay excess labour earnings through higher food prices since 1973. This created needless upward pressure on food prices, which in turn contributed to overall inflationary pressures.

Table 2-3 together with the regression results on the average contribution of technological change from Volume I, Table D-3, reveal that the average productivity of capital in this industry was relatively low after 1946 and decreased slightly during the 1973-77 subperiod. In general, it was about the same as the sector's throughout the various periods. From 1970 to 1977 it ranked twelfth in the sector with average capital productivity of 0.90, while it declined during the 1973-77 subperiod to thirteenth position in the sector. These results are confirmed by the regression test in the VES function showing a statistically insignificant average contribution of technological progress to total productivity. On the margin, however, average productivity of capital declined continuously in the industry and considerably more than the average decline for the sector. After 1973 the annual rate of decline in the productivity of capital was much slower than the average for the sector, exhibiting the second slowest rate of decline among all industries (see Volume I, Table 3-27).

In spite of high rate of capital intensity, only the 1960-70 period shows an increase in capital-using technology. One way to explain the effectiveness of new technology on the increase in labour productivity (or labour efficiency) is to utilize the m coefficient of the VES production function. We see that the food and beverage industries possess a relatively small m coefficient, ranking twelfth out of the nineteen industries of the sector. This means that capital is not highly complementary to labour efficiency and that an injection of new capital to this industry will not significantly affect the level of labour efficiency unless new production technologies are introduced simultaneously. Seemingly the R & D in the industry was not highly effective in promoting capital productivity.

Figure 2-3 verifies these findings. It shows the share of labour in value added output to be relatively unchanged from 1946 to 1960, to

FIGURE 2-3
RATE OF EARNINGS AND LABOUR SHARE OF VALUE ADDED, FOOD AND BEVERAGE PRODUCTS INDUSTRIES
(in 1971 constant dollars)

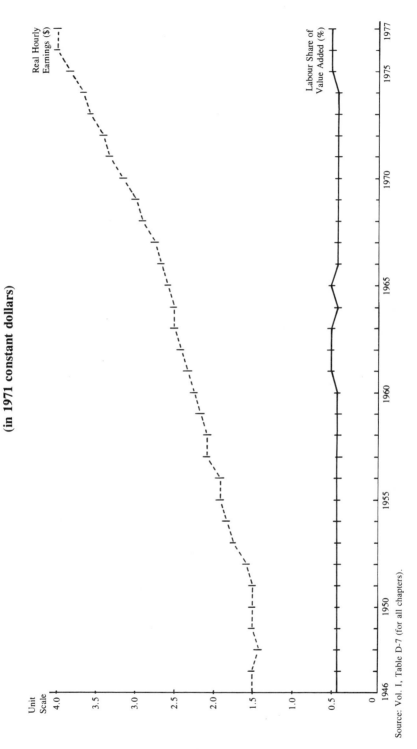

Source: Vol. I, Table D-7 (for all chapters).

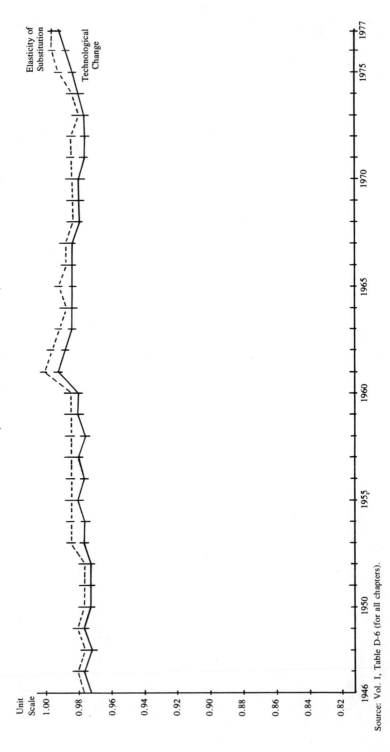

FIGURE 2-4

ELASTICITY OF SUBSTITUTION AND TECHNOLOGICAL CHANGE, FOOD AND BEVERAGE PRODUCTS INDUSTRIES

(in 1971 constant dollars)

Source: Vol. I, Table D-6 (for all chapters).

increase slightly between 1960 and 1966, and to fall back to previous levels until 1974. From 1974 until 1977 the labour share increased, implying a decrease in the share of capital in value added. Real earnings per hour paid increased significantly between 1957 and 1976, when the rate of change decreased sharply only in the sub-period 1973-77.

Figure 2-4 shows two variables representing labour-using or capital-using technology, and the ease with which these production factors could substitute for each other while maintaining the same level of output. This is called the variable elasticity of substitution (VES) of the biased type. The two variables are different, however related or consistent with each other. After 1946 the value of the technological progress variable was slightly below one, indicating that the production technology used by the industry was slightly capital using or labour saving. After 1960 there was a trend of increasing labour-using or capital-saving technology, a slight decline from the situation in the 1961-71 period; the trend reversed in 1971. The variables are consistent because when the industry is using less capital-intensive technology, the ease of substitution between labour and capital increases.

The last issue to be analysed is the impact of economies of scale on productivity. This industry enjoyed relatively strong economies of scale — only seven industries had greater economies of scale than this industry — of 1.4 to 1.5. Figure 2-2 shows that the economies of scale variable (or elasticity of scale) changed only slightly in thirty-two years. A further test, using the Translog production function, shows that the scale elasticity in this industry increased at an increasing rate, though in a statistically insignificant way. The results from the CES and the Translog functions are consistent: they show that economies of scale contributed very little to labour productivity. Another test of the validity of these results is the Diwan method, which calculates the contribution to growth in labour productivity from economies of scale and from "all other factors." The results of this test are perfectly consistent with the previous results: they show that economies of scale contributed only 7 per cent to growth in labour productivity (see Volume I, Table 3-10) in the food and beverages industry.

Tobacco Products Industries 3

The tobacco products industry group contributes 1 per cent of the value added by the manufacturing sector. It is concentrated in twenty-four establishments employing 6,125 workers. The value added by employees in each establishment is the highest in the manufacturing sector.

Capacity Utilization

Figure 3-1 shows that the industry stayed close to full capacity operation from 1953 to 1967, producing at its full capacity in 1956. Capacity utilization dropped to 86.6 per cent in 1968 and increased back to 91 per cent in 1973. By 1977 the industry utilized 95 per cent of its capacity. Comparing the industry with total manufacturing, we see that the annual rate of growth in capacity utilization during the 1950s was 0.9 per cent, while in total manufacturing it was 0.02 per cent. In the 1960s utilization in the tobacco industry declined at an annual rate of 0.7 per cent, whereas that in total manufacturing increased by 1.2 per cent per year. In the 1970s the industry's annual capacity utilization rate rose by 1.0 per cent, while that in total manufacturing fell at 0.34 per cent. Since full capacity utilization implies optimum allocation of production resources, this industry scores quite high compared with industries with lower capacity utilization.

Labour Productivity, Capital Intensity, Real Earnings, and Economies of Scale

Table 3-1 shows the industry's average performance compared with that in total manufacturing. The tobacco products industry outperformed the manufacturing sector significantly in average labour

16

FIGURE 3-1
CAPACITY UTILIZATION, TOBACCO PRODUCTS INDUSTRIES
(in 1971 constant dollars)

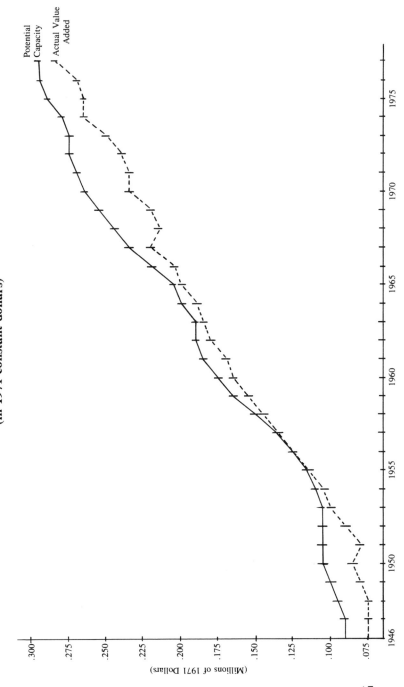

TABLE 3-1

AVERAGE ANNUAL PERFORMANCE OF LABOUR PRODUCTIVITY,
CAPITAL INTENSITY, AND REAL EARNINGS,
TOBACCO PRODUCTS INDUSTRIES

	Tobacco Products	Total Manu.	Industry/ Sector
	(1971 $/hour)		(%)
Labour Productivity			
1946-77	8.49	4.93	172.2
1946-60	5.05	3.50	144.3
1960-70	9.65	5.34	180.7
1970-77	14.15	7.43	190.4
1973-77	15.09	7.79	193.7
Capital Intensity			
1946-77	5.07	5.58	90.9
1946-60	3.23	4.47	72.3
1960-70	5.80	6.67	87.0
1970-77	7.98	9.11	87.6
1973-77	8.28	9.53	86.9
Real Earnings			
1946-77	2.92	2.75	106.2
1946-60	1.96	2.07	94.7
1960-70	3.15	2.96	106.4
1970-77	4.47	3.79	117.9
1973-77	4.66	3.92	118.9

productivity throughout all the periods, while being continuously below the sector average in capital intensity. The recent argument that the main cause of the productivity slowdown is the declining ratio of capital to man-hour of labour clearly does not hold in this industry. While average labour productivity tripled since the 1950s, and was always about twice the sector's average, average capital intensity increased during the same three decades only slightly more than one and a half times, which was always below the sector average. Average real earnings per hour increased throughout the period and remained above the sector average after 1960. This increase in average real earnings in the tobacco industry was, however, smaller than that of labour productivity.

Annual compounded rates of change are outlined in Tables 3-2 and 3-3 and in Figures 3-2, 3-3, and 3-4. Table 3-2 shows that the annual rate of growth in labour productivity decreased from 7.32 per cent in

TABLE 3-2

**COMPOUNDED ANNUAL RATES OF CHANGE IN LABOUR
PRODUCTIVITY, CAPITAL INTENSITY, AND REAL EARNINGS,
TOBACCO PRODUCTS INDUSTRIES**

(% in 1971 constant dollars)

	Tobacco Products	Total Manu.	Industry/ Sector
Labour Productivity			
1946-77	5.68	3.70	153.5
1946-60	7.32	3.82	191.6
1960-70	3.94	3.64	108.2
1970-77	4.92	3.53	139.4
1970-73	5.10	5.04	101.2
1973-77	4.78	2.41	198.3
Capital Intensity			
1946-77	4.66	3.83	121.7
1946-60	6.34	4.99	127.1
1960-70	3.58	2.34	153.0
1970-77	2.92	3.66	79.8
1970-73	3.48	1.90	183.2
1973-77	2.50	5.01	49.9
Real Earnings			
1946-77	4.32	2.85	151.6
1946-60	4.82	3.27	147.4
1960-70	4.37	2.94	148.6
1970-77	3.90	2.31	168.8
1970-73	4.09	2.72	150.4
1973-77	3.75	2.01	186.6

the 1950s to 3.94 per cent in the 1960s. The annual rate of decline in capital intensity was similar for the same period, but real earnings declined by only 10 per cent. In the 1970-77 period labour productivity increased by 25 per cent, while real earnings decreased by 12 per cent and capital intensity decreased by about 23 per cent. Table 3-2 shows a decline in all three variables for the post-energy crisis period, although because the decline is computed only for four years it is not certain whether it is a "true" decline of 23 per cent, or whether the relatively large expected random error is causing such a change. Nevertheless, a structural break attributable to the energy crisis is not apparent in this industry group.

Figure 3-2 depicts the relationships among the rates of change of labour productivity, capital intensity, real earnings, and economies of scale. It shows that throughout the period the rate of change in labour productivity was greater than that for capital intensity and earnings per man-hour. Economies of scale show stability since 1958, and the CD and CES tests placed this industry with the highest economies of scale in the sector (1.92). The Translog production function shows that the industry enjoyed economies of scale, but to a lesser extent (1.07), while maintaining stability through time. I do not believe the results from the Translog function are more reliable than those from the CD and the CES functions, because the time series tested was too short (1958-77) for this function and the results reject the possibility of the non-hometheticity of the production function. I am more inclined, therefore, to accept the results from the usual neoclassical functions. The industry enjoyed significant economies of scale, and 30 per cent of the growth in labour productivity in this industry is attributable to the

FIGURE 3-2
RATES OF CHANGE IN LABOUR PRODUCTIVITY, CAPITAL INTENSITY, REAL EARNINGS, AND ECONOMIES OF SCALE, TOBACCO PRODUCTS INDUSTRIES
(in 1971 constant dollars)

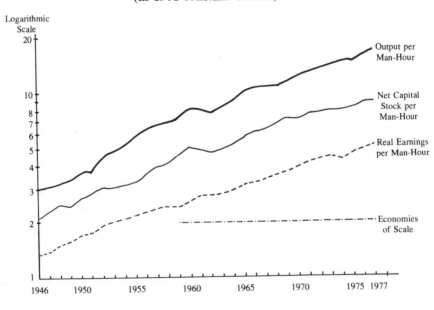

20

TABLE 3 -3

RATIO OF LABOUR PRODUCTIVITY/EARNINGS, OUTPUT/CAPITAL, AND
TECHNOLOGICAL CHANGE,
TOBACCO PRODUCTS INDUSTRIES

(in 1971 constant dollars)

	1946-77	1946-60	1960-70	1970-77	1970-73	1973-77
	AVERAGE LABOUR PRODUCTIVITY/AVERAGE REAL EARNINGS					
Total manufacturing	1.79	1.69	1.80	1.96		1.99
Tobacco	2.91	2.58	3.06	3.17		3.24
	COMPOUNDED RATES OF CHANGE IN LABOUR PRODUCTIVITY/REAL EARNINGS					
Total manufacturing	1.30	1.17	1.24	1.53	1.85	1.20
Tobacco	1.32	1.52	0.90	1.26	1.25	1.28
	AVERAGE OUTPUT/AVERAGE CAPITAL					
Total manufacturing	0.81	0.80	0.81	0.82	0.83	0.82
Tobacco	1.70	n.a.	1.67	1.71	1.71	1.82
	COMPOUNDED RATES OF CHANGE IN OUTPUT/CAPITAL					
Total manufacturing	−0.14	−1.14	1.30	−0.16	2.95	−2.43
Tobacco	n.a.	n.a.	0.36	1.93	1.58	2.19

	COMPOUNDED RATES OF CHANGE IN TECHNOLOGY (%)		
	1946-77	1960-70	1970-77
Total manufacturing	0.271	0.259	0.361
Tobacco	−0.359	0.146	−0.419

existing economies of scale. Furthermore, the impact of technology on labour efficiency (Table 3-8, Vol. I) is the third highest in the sector at 1.8, meaning that a 1 per cent improvement in technology generates 1.8 per cent improvement in labour efficiency. Such an improvement in labour efficiency is reflected in an increase in labour productivity.

Table 3-3 compares explicit structural relationships in this industry with those in total manufacturing. On average, it appears that labour productivity was about three times as high as the real earnings paid for labour in this industry and about 1.60 times higher than the sector average. Thus labour received only one-third of its contribution to productivity.

For policy purposes, it is far more useful to see whether increases in the rate of productivity growth were followed by a comparable rise in real earnings. Table 3-2 shows that for the thirty-two year period from 1946 to 1977, the rate of productivity growth was 1.32 greater than the rate of growth in real earnings per hour. In the 1946-60 period the rate

21

FIGURE 3-3
ELASTICITY OF SUBSTITUTION AND TECHNOLOGICAL
CHANGE, TOBACCO PRODUCTS INDUSTRIES
(in 1971 constant dollars)

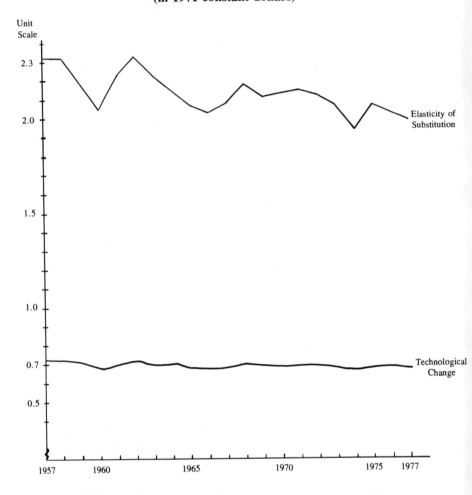

of productivity growth was 1.52 greater than the rate of growth in real earnings, meaning that labour received only 66 per cent of its added contribution to productivity. In the 1960s, however, the rate of increase in real earnings outstripped the rate of growth in labour productivity by 11 per cent, and labour received in hourly earnings more than it increased production. From 1970 to 1977 this situation

22

FIGURE 3-4
RATE OF EARNINGS AND LABOUR SHARE OF VALUE ADDED, TOBACCO PRODUCTS INDUSTRIES
(in 1971 constant dollars)

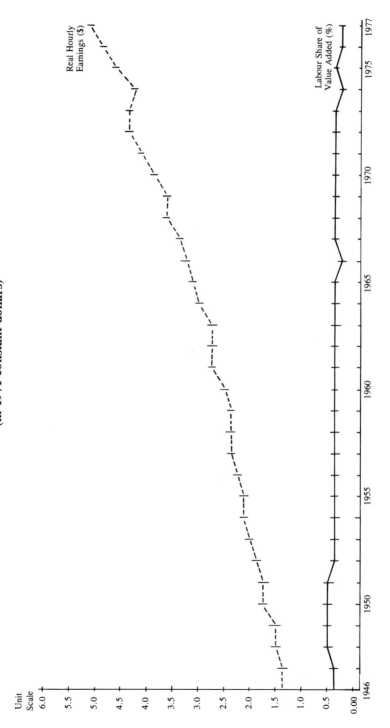

reversed, and only 79 per cent of productivity increases went to labour earnings. Since the demand for tobacco products is relatively price inelastic, the situation in the 1960s does not imply that payment to labour cut into the profit structure of the industry, because consumers paid more than they otherwise would have paid in order to compensate for the gap between productivity and labour earnings.

An examination of Table 3-3 also reveals that the average productivity of capital in this industry in the various periods was consistently double the sectoral average and relatively constant through time. The industry's capital productivity was strong compared with that of the sector: average capital productivity increased over fivefold from the 1960s to the 1970s, while that of the sector declined from 1.30 to −0.16 per cent per year. These findings are consistent with the regression results of the VES function, which showed that technological change contributed 2.4 per cent annually to productivity increases for the 1958-77 period. On the margin, however, the tobacco industry has experienced a 0.42 per cent annual decline in technological progress since 1970.

Figure 3-3 illustrates this pattern of the "non-neutral" technological progress function g. There are two properties to observe here: first, the value of g was less than one all along, which means that the technology in this industry was basically labour-saving or capital-using; second, technological progress was fairly stable up to 1970 and then declined, indicating capital intensification during the 1970s.

The second variable in Figure 3-3 is the elasticity of substitution of the biased type. In the case of the tobacco products industry there are some distinct fluctuations in the elasticity of substitution variable throughout the period, but a decrease from almost 3 to around 2 is noticeable. This suggests that the production technology in this industry was such that labour and capital could be substituted with relative ease without impairing productivity and output levels. But an examination of Figure 3-4 shows quite clearly that historically this was not the case, since labour's share of value added was relatively stable from 1957 to 1965, then dropped slightly from 1965 to 1967, and then dropped again in the 1973-75 period. If historical tendencies continue, the share of labour will continue to decline slightly in the future, as the use of capital intensifies in line with the technological progress function. Real hourly earnings rose at an accelerated rate after 1973.

Rubber and Plastic Products Industries

4

The products of this industry group, which represents 3.1 per cent of the sector value added and consists of 776 establishments, are diverse. The value added per establishment places it ninth in the sector; by number of employees it ranks eleventh.

Capacity Utilization

Figure 4-1 shows the gap between actual and potential output, given the industry's available resources. Full capacity utilization was reached in 1947 and after that there was a continuous decrease in the utilization rate. The lowest capacity utilization was achieved in 1954, 1961, and 1975. The last two years happen to conform with low points in the index of industrial production, but the industry's capacity fluctuations throughout the thirty-two-year period do not resemble the fluctuations in that index, and it is therefore difficult to relate in general this industry's fluctuations to the sector's. Again when compounded annual rates of change in capacity utilization are computed, this industry shows a different pattern than the sector.

Although in absolute terms capacity utilization levels in total manufacturing were higher all along than those of the industry, the comparative rates of change reveal an interesting phenomenon. Following a significant decline in the 1950s the industry picked up quite strongly during the 1960s (Table 4-1). In the 1970s there was a significant decline in the manufacturing sector's capacity utilization rate, whereas the rubber and plastic products industry continued to increase capacity utilization by 1 per cent annually. This growth was greatest between 1970 and 1973, slowing afterwards to 0.6 per cent annually. Since this is high-energy content industry, a more severe decline in the capacity utilization rate might have occurred. One reason that did not happen might be that the demand for rubber and plastic products is relatively price inelastic and therefore the industry could

25

FIGURE 4-1
CAPACITY UTILIZATION, RUBBER AND PLASTIC PRODUCTS INDUSTRIES
(in 1971 constant dollars)

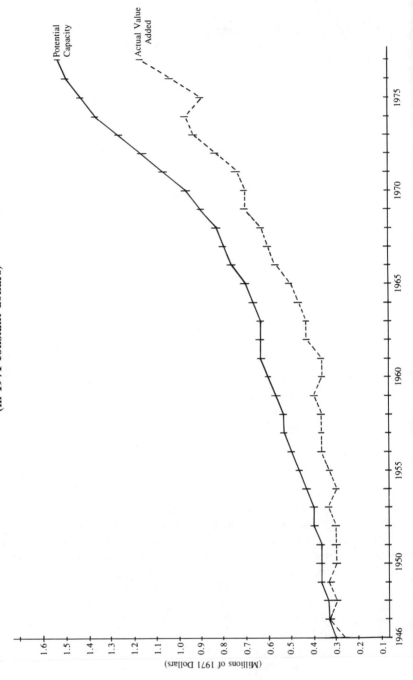

26

TABLE 4-1

COMPOUNDED ANNUAL RATES OF GROWTH
IN CAPACITY UTILIZATION,
RUBBER AND PLASTIC PRODUCTS INDUSTRIES

	1946-60	1960-70	1970-73	1973-77
Total manufacturing	0.02	1.15	−0.34	−2.57
Rubber and Plastic	−2.88	2.94	1.05	0.61

increase its output with appropriate adjustments for energy price increases, which were paid for primarily by the final consumers. This industry group was operating in 1976 at 67.9 per cent of capacity and in 1977 at 75.2 per cent. The 25 per cent idle excess capacity could probably be utilized with further capital investment.

Labour Productivity, Capital Intensity, Real Earnings, and Economies of Scale

Figure 4-2 shows the rate of change of labour productivity, capital intensity, real earnings, and economies of scale.

FIGURE 4-2
RATES OF CHANGE IN LABOUR PRODUCTIVITY, CAPITAL INTENSITY, REAL EARNINGS, AND ECONOMIES OF SCALE, RUBBER AND PLASTIC PRODUCTS INDUSTRIES
(in 1971 constant dollars)

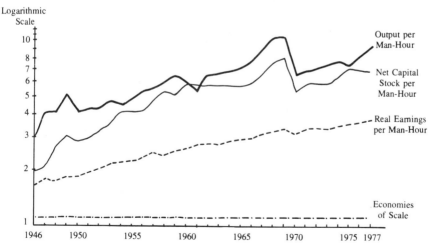

In the rubber and plastic products industry, productivity and capital intensity seem to be consistent from 1946 to 1959, to have diverged from 1959 to 1962, and to be consistent again from 1962 to 1973; from 1973 to 1977 the rate of growth of productivity increased while that of capital intensity decreased. Real earnings per hour increased throughout the whole period with no relationship to fluctuations in productivity, although the rate of growth in real earnings was slower than that of productivity throughout the period. Economies of scale increased slightly from 1.12 in 1946 to 1.14 in 1977, indicating that there was no significant change in the scope of production during the period and that advances in productivity are not related to scale in this industry.

Tables 4-2 and 4-3 give far more specific magnitudes and rates of change of three variables. Average annual labour productivity for the industry was consistently higher than that in the sector from 1946 to

TABLE 4-2

AVERAGE ANNUAL PERFORMANCE OF LABOUR PRODUCTIVITY, CAPITAL INTENSITY, AND REAL EARNINGS, RUBBER AND PLASTIC PRODUCTS INDUSTRIES

	Rubber and Plastic	Total Manu.	Industry/ Sector
	(1971 $/hour)		(%)
Labour Productivity			
1946-77	6.27	4.93	127.18
1946-60	4.80	3.50	137.14
1960-70	7.55	5.34	141.39
1970-77	7.57	7.43	101.88
1973-77	8.01	7.79	102.82
Capital Intensity			
1946-77	5.05	5.58	90.50
1946-60	3.74	4.47	83.67
1960-70	6.14	6.67	92.05
1970-77	6.31	9.11	69.26
1973-77	6.66	9.53	69.88
Real Earnings			
1946-77	2.70	2.75	98.18
1946-60	2.13	2.07	102.90
1960-70	2.97	2.96	100.34
1970-77	3.46	3.79	91.29
1973-77	3.56	3.92	90.82

TABLE 4-3

COMPOUNDED ANNUAL RATES OF CHANGE IN LABOUR PRODUCTIVITY, CAPITAL INTENSITY, AND REAL EARNINGS, RUBBER AND PLASTIC PRODUCTS INDUSTRIES

(% in 1971 constant dollars)

	Rubber and Plastic	Total Manu.	Industry/ Sector
Labour Productivity			
1946-77	3.77	3.70	101.89
1946-60	5.04	3.82	131.94
1960-70	0.98	3.64	26.92
1970-77	5.30	3.53	150.14
1970-73	3.83	5.04	75.99
1973-77	6.42	2.41	266.39
Capital Intensity			
1946-77	4.14	3.83	108.09
1946-60	8.15	4.99	163.33
1960-70	-0.97	2.34	41.45
1970-77	3.73	3.66	101.91
1970-73	4.07	1.90	214.2
1973-77	3.29	5.01	65.7
Real Earnings			
1946-77	2.59	2.85	90.88
1946-60	3.38	3.27	103.36
1960-70	2.03	2.94	69.05
1970-77	2.22	2.31	96.10
1970-73	1.95	2.72	71.69
1973-77	2.43	2.01	120.90

1970; in the 1970s the industry's average productivity converged with that of the sector. Average capital intensity performance was quite different. First, the industry's capital intensity was always below the sectoral average, ranging from 92 per cent to 70 per cent of the sector level. Average real earnings were on par with the average earnings in the sector in the 1950s and the 1960s, and slightly below it in the 1970s.

Table 4-4 provides some complementary information, showing first that average annual labour productivity was well over twice the average hourly labour earnings. In the 1950s labour produced 2.3 times its earnings; during the 1960s it produced 2.6 times its hourly earnings; and in the 1970s, 2.2 times. An examination of Table 3-16 in

TABLE 4-4

RATIO OF LABOUR PRODUCTIVITY/EARNINGS, OUTPUT/CAPITAL, AND TECHNOLOGICAL CHANGE, RUBBER AND PLASTIC PRODUCTS INDUSTRIES

(in 1971 constant dollars)

	1946-77	1946-60	1960-70	1970-77	1970-73	1973-77
AVERAGE LABOUR PRODUCTIVITY/AVERAGE REAL EARNINGS						
Total manufacturing	1.79	1.69	1.80	1.96		1.99
Rubber and Plastic	2.32	2.25	2.56	2.19		2.25
COMPOUNDED RATES OF CHANGE IN LABOUR PRODUCTIVITY/REAL EARNINGS						
Total manufacturing	1.30	1.17	1.24	1.53	1.85	1.20
Rubber and Plastic	1.46	1.49	0.48	2.39	1.96	2.64
AVERAGE OUTPUT/AVERAGE CAPITAL						
Total manufacturing	0.81	0.80	0.81	0.82	0.83	0.82
Rubber and Plastic	1.28	1.34	1.24	1.20	0.90	1.21
COMPOUNDED RATES OF CHANGE IN OUTPUT/CAPITAL						
Total manufacturing	−0.14	−1.14	1.30	−0.16	2.95	−2.43
Rubber and Plastic	−0.35	−2.88	1.96	1.52	0.59	2.22

COMPOUNDED RATES OF CHANGE IN TECHNOLOGY (%)		
	1946-77	1960-70	1970-77
Total manufacturing	0.27	0.26	0.36
Rubber and Plastic	0.03	0.10	−1.39

Volume I shows that the absolute real hourly earnings in this industry ranked the sixth lowest in the sector, well below the sectoral average. The average productivity of capital (output-capital ratio) in the sector was rather stable throughout at about 0.8, while the industry average fluctuated between 1.2 and 1.34. Dividing the 1970-77 period into two subperiods shows that the average productivity of capital was higher in the post-energy crisis period. Altogether this industry group had lower than average capital intensity with greater than average labour productivity and among the lowest average real earnings per hour. But the industry did have favourable average capital productivity.

The regression results in Tables D-3 and D-4 (Vol. I) indicate an average contribution of technical change to total factor productivity of 2.3 per cent per year. It is therefore important to measure the impact of new technology on labour efficiency in this industry. The m coefficient of the VES production function is a measure of elasticity that reflects the productivity of new technology. If m were zero, labour efficiency was not dependent on capital. The value of this coefficient is 0.85, showing that capital was not highly complementary to labour efficiency. These results are consistent with our findings that this industry had low capital intensity with more than proportionate productivity performance.

The compounded rates of change of these variables show the dynamic development in the industry that is generally crucial for policy formation. Table 4-3 shows that labour productivity per man-hour increased from 5.04 in the 1950s to 5.30 in the 1970s, declining to 3.83 in 1970-73 and rising to 6.42 in 1973-77. The significant drop in the 1960s seems inconsistent with the general behaviour of the series and was probably caused by a data problem rather than a structural break. The rate of change in total manufacturing was lower than that of the industry in all periods with the exception of the 1970-73 subperiod. The rate of change in real earnings per hour was above the sectoral rate of change only in the 1950s and in 1973-77. On the margin, the rate of change in labour productivity exceeded the rate of change in hourly earnings by 1.5 in the 1950s, by 2.0 in the 1960s, and by 2.4 in the 1970s. The rate of change in capital intensity was above the sectoral rate of change in the 1950s and in the 1970s and below that in the 1960s. The marginal productivity of capital was negative in the 1950s but positive and above the sectoral rate in the 1960s and 1970s. Particularly strong performance occurred during the 1973-77 subperiod. This industry group maintained tenth place in the sector with respect to the average productivity of capital; however, it was in third place with respect to the rate of change of productivity of capital in the 1970s.

Technological advances in this industry were distinctly stronger in the 1970-77 period than in the previous two decades, moving in the opposite direction from the manufacturing sector and at a much higher annual rate. Figure 4-3 reflects that in 1976 the industry took on new

FIGURE 4 -3
ELASTICITY OF SUBSTITUTION AND TECHNOLOGICAL CHANGE, RUBBER AND PLASTIC PRODUCTS INDUSTRIES
(in 1971 constant dollars)

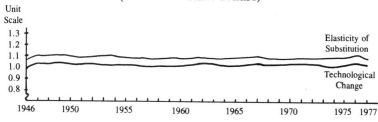

31

FIGURE 4-4
RATE OF EARNINGS AND LABOUR SHARE OF VALUE ADDED, RUBBER AND PLASTIC PRODUCTS INDUSTRIES
(in 1971 constant dollars)

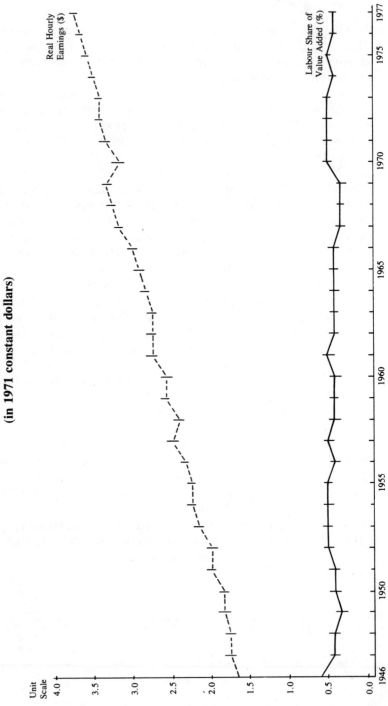

capital-using technology, after a long stable period with few changes in technology. The variable elasticity of substitution of the biased type, computed from the VES production function, is consistent with this pattern. The value of the variable remained about one up to 1976, meaning that substitution was relatively easy, but after 1976 substitution became more difficult because the factors of production became too dissimilar.

Figure 4-4 supports that analysis. It shows that real earnings per hour fluctuated somewhat throughout the period, although along a rising trend. Labour's share of value added by this industry increased in the 1950-55 period, remained almost the same until 1966 when it declined until 1969, to rise again between 1969 and 1973 and decline after 1974. Stronger technological progress after 1975 resulted in a decreasing trend of labour share of value added because payments to capital as factor of production increased. For the whole period, however, the impact of technological change on total factor productivity was the lowest in the sector.

To relate the change in economies of scale to productivity in this industry, I employed two methods. The Diwan method shows clearly that there was no growth in labour productivity that could be attributed to economies of scale (see Volume I, Table 3-10); in fact the contribution of scale to productivity growth was negative, meaning that the rationalization of size and products and the internalization of intraindustry externalities should be priority items on the industry's strategic planning agenda. The second test, derived from the estimation of the Translog production function, showed (see Volume I, Table 3-6) that the industry experienced economies of scale of 1.06 and that scale economies were finally showing at the end of the 1970s.

The prognosis for the industry is cautiously optimistic given that the industry will continue the process of technological improvement begun in the mid-1970s. But the rubber and plastic products industry will still have to rationalize its product mix and runs, scale, and technology in order to become truly competitive. This process of rationalization is fundamental to the industry's structure and future performance in a competitive environment. Improved productivity would enhance productivity improvement in closely related industries such as the leather industry, which relies heavily on rubber products.

Leather Products Industries

5

Capacity Utilization

Figure 5-1 shows the gap between actual and potential output given the leather products industries' available resources. The fluctuations in the capacity utilization rate in this industry group were quite pronounced throughout the period. The industry operated at full capacity in 1946, at 68 per cent in 1961, and at a high of 98.8 per cent in 1965. The decline in capacity utilization continued after 1967 to reach a 76 per cent utilization rate in 1977 (Figure 5-1). The utilization pattern in this industry was entirely different from that of the sector, which followed the V-shape up to 1976. The capacity utilization rate in the sector converged with the potential rate in 1965. From 1970 until 1973 the industry's rate of decline was 1.38 per cent per annum greater than the sectoral rate of decline; from 1973 the industry followed the sectoral annual rate of decline.

Extensive discussions with people in the leather industry revealed that Statistics Canada capital stock figures for this industry are biased downward considerably. This is *not* because Statistics Canada survey methods are faulty but because the industry leases close to 50 per cent of its capital equipment and, therefore, by the national accounts definition, the cost of the leased capital stock appears as an annual operating expense and never enters the capital stock category. Consequently, the *real* gap between actual and potential output for this industry was far larger than displayed, and thus its capacity utilization rate was actually much lower.

Labour Productivity, Capital Intensity, Real Earnings, and Economies of Scale

Table 5-1 displays the average performance for the leather industry in labour productivity, capital intensity, and real earnings. Average annual labour productivity for the industry consistently ranged from 53

34

FIGURE 5-1
CAPACITY UTILIZATION, LEATHER PRODUCTS INDUSTRIES
(in 1971 constant dollars)

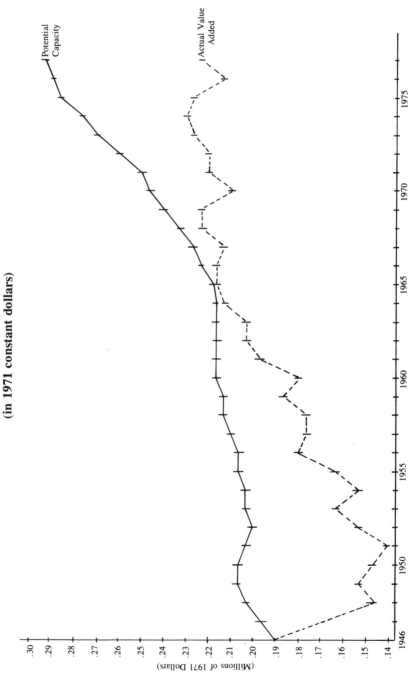

35

TABLE 5-1

**AVERAGE ANNUAL PERFORMANCE OF LABOUR PRODUCTIVITY,
CAPITAL INTENSITY, AND REAL EARNINGS,
LEATHER PRODUCTS INDUSTRIES**

	Leather	Total Manu.	Industry/ Sector
	(1971 $/hour)		(%)
Labour Productivity			
1946-77	3.09	4.93	63.0
1946-60	2.46	3.50	70.0
1960-70	3.23	5.34	60.0
1970-77	4.26	7.43	57.0
1973-77	4.46	7.79	57.0
Capital Intensity			
1946-77	1.46	5.58	26.0
1946-60	1.30	4.47	29.0
1960-70	1.35	6.67	20.0
1970-77	1.98	9.11	22.0
1973-77	2.12	9.53	22.0
Real Earnings			
1946-77	2.00	2.75	73.0
1946-60	1.56	2.07	75.0
1960-70	2.09	2.96	71.0
1970-77	2.72	3.79	72.0
1973-77	2.87	3.92	73.0

per cent to 70 per cent below the sectoral average, although average
productivity did increase in the early 1970s as well as after 1973.

A glance at the capital intensity category shows that although
average capital intensity increased from 1.3 in the 1946-60 period to
2.1 in the 1973-77 period, the industry remained far less capital
intensive than the sector. Overall, the industry is not capital intensive,
and the average rates of increase in productivity are consistent with the
capital-intensity rates — even if production technology in this industry
is more capital intensive than shown because of capital leasing
practices.

This industry managed to maintain a stable relationship between
average real earnings and productivity over the whole period. Workers
produced on average one and a half times their average earnings. Thus
they were compensated on average for far less than they contributed to
average productivity growth and cannot be accused of overcharging
their employers for their services.

36

Tables 5-2 and 5-3 and Figure 5-2 focus attention on rates of change in labour productivity, capital intensity, and real earnings, which were either a consequence of market forces or public policies that affected (positively or negatively) performance through time. Table 5-2 shows that labour productivity per man-hour increased from 1.59 per annum in the 1956-60 period to 4.39 per annum between 1973 and 1977. Two observations are noteworthy here. First, labour productivity in this industry rose from 41.6 per cent of the sectoral rate to almost *twice* the rate of performance in the sector. Second, the decrease in the rate of growth in productivity occurred in the 1970-73 period. After 1973 the rate of annual productivity growth increased by half of a percentage point, while that in total manufacturing experienced an annual drop in

TABLE 5-2

COMPOUNDED ANNUAL RATES OF CHANGE IN LABOUR PRODUCTIVITY, CAPITAL INTENSITY, AND REAL EARNINGS, LEATHER PRODUCTS INDUSTRIES

(% in 1971 constant dollars)

	Leather	Total Manu.	Industry/ Sector
Labour Productivity			
1946-77	2.52	3.70	68.1
1946-60	1.59	3.82	41.6
1960-70	2.70	3.64	74.2
1970-77	4.16	3.53	117.8
1970-73	3.84	5.04	76.8
1973-77	4.39	2.41	182.2
Capital Intensity			
1946-77	2.72	3.83	71.0
1946-60	1.88	4.99	37.7
1960-70	2.33	2.34	99.6
1970-77	4.99	3.66	136.3
1970-73	4.32	1.90	227.4
1973-77	5.49	5.01	109.6
Real Earnings			
1946-77	2.71	2.85	95.1
1946-60	2.17	3.27	66.4
1960-70	2.90	2.94	98.6
1970-77	3.52	2.31	152.4
1970-73	2.82	2.72	103.7
1973-77	4.04	2.01	201.0

FIGURE 5-2

RATES OF CHANGE IN LABOUR PRODUCTIVITY, CAPITAL INTENSITY, REAL EARNINGS, AND ECONOMIES OF SCALE, LEATHER PRODUCTS INDUSTRIES
(in 1971 constant dollars)

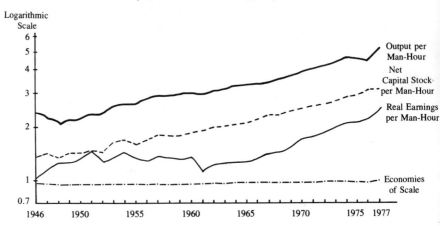

labour productivity of 2.5 percentage points. The capital intensity pattern followed a similar pattern accelerating from 1.88 per cent per annum during the 1946-60 period to a rate of 5.49 per cent in the 1973-77 subperiod. The increase during the latest subperiod was about one-half a percentage point higher than that of the sector. In neither case did the energy crisis affect the rate of capital intensification.

One way to explain the increased productivity is to test the impact of new technology on labour efficiency in this industry by computing the *m* coefficient of the VES production function. From Table 3-8 in Volume I we see that the leather industries possessed the largest coefficient in the manufacturing sector. Labour efficiency was therefore highly complementary to new technology, and the growth in productivity could be attributed partially to the new leased technology practices of this industry. The technological progress function shows the leather industry to be slightly more labour intensive, and complementary injections of new technology could increase employment and productivity simultaneously in this industry. Since the industry is regionally concentrated, it is imperative that governments are aware that local employment could be increased by aiding this industry to expand.

Government policy should also take into account the marginal growth rates in real hourly earnings in the varied periods, since they differ considerably from the averages. For example, in the 1946-60 and 1960-70 periods the growth in labour wages and salaries outstripped the annual growth in productivity. Furthermore, Table 3-23 in Volume I shows that during the last three decades the industry paid labour somewhat above its marginal productivity, and this of course must have created some upward pressure on the price of leather products in the market place. Neither labour nor management should be criticized for this, because the marginal productivity in this industry was so low during these two periods that labour would have had to be subsidized by the government in order to maintain a minimal standard of living. Instead, this industry was subsidized by consumers, because the price elasticity of demand for shoes is rather low, and producers passed the cost of the excess wage paid to labour on to consumers in order to maintain a secure level of profit.

Table 5-3 shows as well that from 1970 on this trend changed considerably. Workers' hourly productivity increased from 1970 to

TABLE 5-3

RATIO OF LABOUR PRODUCTIVITY/EARNINGS, OUTPUT/CAPITAL, AND TECHNOLOGICAL CHANGE, LEATHER PRODUCTS INDUSTRIES

(in 1971 constant dollars)

	1946-77	1946-60	1960-70	1970-77	1970-73	1973-77
	AVERAGE LABOUR PRODUCTIVITY/AVERAGE REAL EARNINGS					
Total manufacturing	1.79	1.69	1.80	1.96		1.99
Leather	1.55	1.58	1.55	1.57		1.55
	COMPOUNDED RATES OF CHANGE IN LABOUR PRODUCTIVITY/REAL EARNINGS					
Total manufacturing	1.30	1.17	1.24	1.53	1.85	1.20
Leather	0.93	0.73	0.93	1.18	1.36	1.09
	AVERAGE OUTPUT/AVERAGE CAPITAL					
Total manufacturing	0.81	0.80	0.81	0.82	0.83	0.82
Leather	2.12	1.90	2.42	2.16	2.23	1.67
	COMPOUNDED RATES OF CHANGE IN OUTPUT/CAPITAL					
Total manufacturing	0.13	1.15	−1.27	0.15	−3.0	2.57
Leather	0.20	0.30	−0.37	0.80	0.59	0.97
	COMPOUNDED RATES OF CHANGE IN TECHNOLOGY (%)					
	1946-77	1960-70	1970-77			
Total manufacturing	0.271	0.259	0.361			
Leather	−0.003	−0.010	0.014			

1977 by 27 per cent (compared with 1960-70) relative to their hourly earnings. This trend was stronger in the 1970-73 subperiod when workers' productivity growth was 36 per cent *above* the rate of increase in earnings. This, of course, should have a positive effect on the profit structure of this industry and its price competitiveness in the market. In the 1973-77 period the rate of change in real earnings converged to "normal" and conformed with a classic situation; workers received in increased earnings the equivalent of their increased productivity.

An examination of Table 5-3 together with the regression results on technological improvement in Table D-3 of Volume I reveals that the average productivity of capital in this industry was relatively high throughout the various periods. From 1970 to 1977, it ranked third in the sector (2.16), slipping to fifth position (1.67) in the 1973-77 subperiod. In all periods the average productivity of capital was at least twice that of total manufacturing. These results are confirmed by the regression tests of the VES, showing that technological progress contributed 1.39 per cent annually to the total productivity growth (see Volume I, Table D-3). However, the marginal productivity of capital in the industry declined, though the rate of decline after 1973 was about one-third of the rate of decrease in the sector and the third slowest among sixteen manufacturing industry groups (see Volume I, Table 3-14).

Technological advances in the industry are reflected in Figure 5-3. The figure shows a relatively stable labour share of value added throughout the three decades, with a small decline from 1968 to 1974, an increase from 1975 to 1976, and then a sharp fall as if a substantial injection of capital occurred. Discussions with executives in the industries and with related R & D personnel confirmed that extensive programs and the implementation of new technology (fully automated computerized machinery) were in progress as part of the government-supported program to develop the industry and increase its competitiveness.

A further important question is how changes in economies of scale relate to productivity in this industry. Again, I employed two methods to test the contribution of scale to productivity and to trace the rate of change in economies of scale. The Diwan method clearly shows that there was no growth in labour productivity that could be attributed to scale elasticity. In fact the contribution to productivity was negative, indicating that a rationalization of size and products and an internalization of intraindustry externalities should be a high item on

FIGURE 5-3
ELASTICITY OF SUBSTITUTION AND TECHNOLOGICAL
CHANGE, LEATHER PRODUCTS INDUSTRIES
(in 1971 constant dollars)

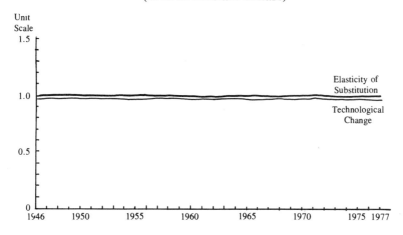

the industry's agenda. Since the firms in this industry are often small or medium sized, and highly automated machinery is designed for large volumes, one way to rationalize production may be to create a pool of users for a given machine. The productivity of new capital would increase dramatically and help the industry achieve the status of an unprotected competitive industry. Needless to say, the Canadian consumer would welcome competitively priced leather products. The second test, which is derived from the estimation of the Translog production function, confirms (see Volume I, Table D-4) that this industry experienced diseconomies of scale that rose insignificantly through time.

The last issue to be examined is the ease with which technology permits capital and labour to be substituted while maintaining the same level of output. Figure 5-4 shows that the variable elasticity of substitution (VES), which takes into account market imperfections, is almost constant through time. Thus factors of production were relatively easily substitutable and technology was almost neutral during the last three decades. Note that the regression results are averages that do not show the 1976 change.

In sum, the results show that the leather products industry would have to rationalize its product mix, scale, and technology in order to become truly competitive. Indeed, a rationalization process is crucial

41

FIGURE 5-4
RATE OF EARNINGS AND LABOUR SHARE OF VALUE ADDED,
LEATHER PRODUCTS INDUSTRIES
(in 1971 constant dollars)

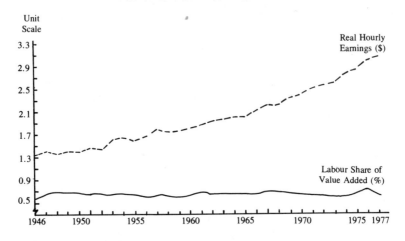

for the industry's structure and future performance in an open, competitive environment. Changes in such basic variables will not be totally accomplished in the short term, but recent technological progress clearly portends a promising future. The international competition the industry faces is severe, and infant industry treatment for an explicitly agreed upon time may be the only way to solve its present inability to compete in the market place. This strategy should, however, be conditional upon the industry guaranteeing to adopt new technology and to rationalize its product mix.

42

Textile Industries
6

This industry group represents 3 per cent of the value added by the manufacturing sector, employs close to 42,000 employees, and contains 890 establishments. It ranks seventh in the sector with respect to employees per establishment, and eleventh with respect to value added per establishment. It is regionally concentrated. The industry has faced severe competition from abroad in recent years and was studied by a special commission that recommended some measures of protection implemented in 1976.

Capacity Utilization

Figure 6-1 shows the industry's potential output plotted against its actual output. Full capacity utilization was reached in 1973, progressing from a low of 61.7 per cent utilization in 1961. From 1973 to 1977 the pattern of capacity utilization fluctuated, dropping to 95.8 per cent in 1974, to 90 per cent in 1975 and 1976, and increasing to 93 per cent in 1977. The increased capacity utilization after 1976 could be an indication that 1976 government measures contributed to increased efficiency in the industry.

A computation of the compounded annual rates of change in capacity utilization places the industry's performance above the sector's. In the 1960s the industry experienced an annual rate of growth in utilization of 2.9 per cent, compared with 1.2 per cent in the sector. In the 1970s the industry's annual rate of growth was 2.2 per cent, versus the rate of −0.3 per cent in the sector. In the 1973-77 subperiod the industry's annual rate of change was −1.8 per cent, compared with −2.6 per cent in the sector.

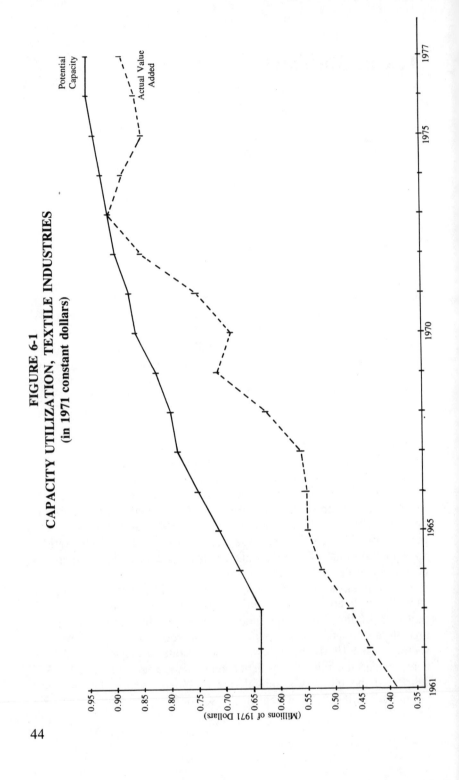

FIGURE 6-1

CAPACITY UTILIZATION, TEXTILE INDUSTRIES

(in 1971 constant dollars)

44

Labour Productivity, Capital Intensity, Real Earnings, and Economies of Scale

Table 6-1 shows the average performance of these three categories in the textile industry group compared with the average in the sector. Labour productivity in the group was 36 per cent below that of the sector for the whole period. In the 1950s the industry's labour productivity was 47 per cent below the sector's; it increased gradually to 77 per cent of the sector's productivity during the 1973-77 subperiod. Capital intensity in the textile industry was also below the sectoral average in all periods, but much closer to it than labour productivity. Average capital intensity in the industry ranged from 97 per cent of the sectoral average in the 1950s to 82 per cent in the 1970s. Hourly real earnings held at around 80 per cent of the sectoral average. Relative to productivity, average earnings were therefore higher in the industry than in the sector, in all sub-periods.

TABLE 6-1

AVERAGE ANNUAL PERFORMANCE OF LABOUR PRODUCTIVITY, CAPITAL INTENSITY, AND REAL EARNINGS, TEXTILE INDUSTRIES

	Textile	Total Manu.	Industry/ Sector
	(1971 $/hour)		(%)
Labour Productivity			
1946-77	3.15	4.93	63.89
1946-60	1.83	3.50	52.29
1960-70	3.43	5.34	64.23
1970-77	5.67	7.43	76.31
1973-77	6.01	7.79	77.15
Capital Intensity			
1946-77	5.41	5.58	96.95
1946-60	4.34	4.47	97.09
1960-70	5.55	6.67	83.21
1970-77	7.49	9.11	82.22
1973-77	7.88	9.53	82.69
Real Earnings			
1946-77	2.22	2.75	80.73
1946-60	1.69	2.07	81.64
1960-70	2.37	2.96	80.07
1970-77	3.05	3.79	80.47
1973-77	3.16	3.92	80.61

TABLE 6-2

COMPOUNDED ANNUAL RATES OF CHANGE IN LABOUR
PRODUCTIVITY, CAPITAL INTENSITY, AND REAL EARNINGS,
TEXTILE INDUSTRIES

(% in 1971 constant dollars)

	Textile	Total Manu.	Industry/ Sector
Labour Productivity			
1946-77	5.01	3.70	135.41
1946-60	4.38	3.82	114.66
1960-70	5.83	3.64	160.16
1970-77	5.11	3.53	144.76
1970-73	6.15	5.04	122.02
1973-77	4.34	2.41	180.08
Capital Intensity			
1946-77	3.39	3.83	88.51
1946-60	4.21	4.99	84.37
1960-70	2.11	2.34	90.17
1970-77	3.59	3.66	98.09
1970-73	7.28	1.90	383.2
1973-77	−1.13	5.01	—
Real Earnings			
1946-77	2.94	2.85	103.16
1946-60	2.78	3.27	85.02
1960-70	3.07	2.94	104.42
1970-77	3.07	2.31	132.90
1970-73	2.24	2.72	82.35
1973-77	3.69	2.01	183.58

Table 6-2 and Figure 6-2 help to analyse the dynamics of the textile industry group. They show the compounded annual rates of change in the three categories.

Table 6-2 shows that the annual rate of increase in labour productivity in the textile industry rose consistently until 1973. From 1973 to 1977 the rise in labour productivity slowed significantly, to the same rate of growth recorded in the 1950s. During the whole period, however, the annual rate of growth in labour productivity in the textile industry rose faster than that in the sector.

The annual rates of growth in real earnings per hour fluctuated somewhat differently from those of labour productivity in the industry and from those in the sector. Figure 6-2 shows clearly that the

FIGURE 6-2

**FIGURE 6-2
RATES OF CHANGE IN LABOUR PRODUCTIVITY, CAPITAL
INTENSITY, REAL EARNINGS, AND ECONOMIES OF SCALE,
TEXTILE INDUSTRIES**
(in 1971 constant dollars)

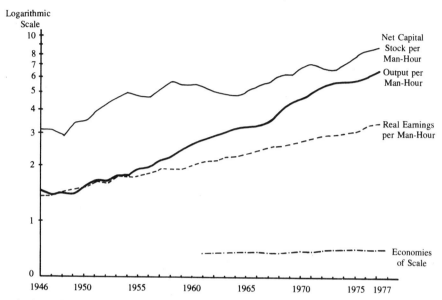

industry's rate of change in real earnings was much smaller than the rate of change in labour productivity, all along the period. Comparing the industry's real earnings changes with those of the sector shows that the real earnings per hour in the industry group grew at the same rate from 1960 to 1973 (3.07 per cent) and this rate of growth was increasingly above the sector's. The sector showed a decline in the rate of growth in the 1970-77 period from 2.94 to 2.31 per cent per annum. In 1970-73, however, there was a significant decline in the industry's annual rate of growth in earnings, while the sector showed an annual increase. This pattern reversed in 1973-77; the yearly rate of growth in real earnings in the industry rose from 2.24 per cent in 1970-73 to 3.69 per cent in 1973-77, while in the sector the growth rate declined from 2.72 per cent to 2.01 per cent for the same periods. This phenomenon presents an inconsistency in the relationship between productivity and earnings in the textile industry; that is, in 1973-77 the rate of growth in productivity declined substantially from the previous period, while real hourly earnings increased considerably. In general, rates of growth in productivity and real earnings should move in the same direction.

TABLE 6-3

RATIO OF LABOUR PRODUCTIVITY/EARNINGS, OUTPUT/CAPITAL, AND TECHNOLOGICAL CHANGE, TEXTILE INDUSTRIES

(in 1971 constant dollars)

	1946-77	1946-60	1960-70	1970-77	1970-73	1973-77
	AVERAGE LABOUR PRODUCTIVITY/AVERAGE REAL EARNINGS					
Total manufacturing	1.79	1.69	1.80	1.96		1.99
Textile	1.42	1.08	1.45	1.86		1.90
	COMPOUNDED RATES OF CHANGE IN LABOUR PRODUCTIVITY/REAL EARNINGS					
Total manufacturing	1.30	1.17	1.24	1.53	1.85	1.20
Textile	1.70	1.58	1.90	1.66	2.46	1.18
	AVERAGE OUTPUT/AVERAGE CAPITAL					
Total manufacturing	0.81	0.80	0.81	0.82	0.83	0.82
Textile	0.69	n.a.	0.63	0.76	0.77	0.77
	COMPOUNDED RATES OF CHANGE IN OUTPUT/CAPITAL					
Total manufacturing	−0.14	−1.14	1.30	−0.16	2.95	−2.43
Textile	n.a.	n.a.	2.87	1.49	7.38	−2.72

	COMPOUNDED RATES OF CHANGE IN TECHNOLOGY (%)		
	1946-77	1960-70	1970-77
Total manufacturing	0.27	0.26	0.36
Textile	2.80	1.86	0.59

Nor are the annual rates of growth in capital intensity consistent with those of productivity growth. In fact, in 1960-70 there was a decline in the rate of growth of capital intensity while, for the same period, the industry showed an increase in the rate of growth in productivity. The 1973-77 subperiod shows a *negative* rate of change in capital intensity following an unprecedented rate of growth of 7.28 per cent per year in 1970-73. The rates of growth in capital intensity of the industry were between 10 and 12 per cent lower than those of the sector. This, however, tells us nothing about the productivity of capital in the industry. Table 6-3 shows that the average productivity of capital was slightly lower than that of the sector throughout the various periods. However, the annual rates of change from 1960 on show that the industry's capital productivity was much higher than the sector's except during the 1973-77 subperiod.

Figure 6-3 shows the trends in real earnings per hour paid and of labour share of output. Real earnings increased steadily until 1970, when growth was above average, followed by a very slight annual

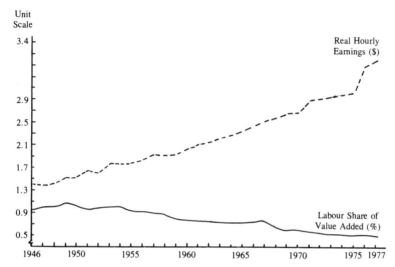

change until 1975, when there was an unprecedented jump in earnings. Labour's share of output declined continuously from 95 per cent in 1946 to 51 per cent in 1977.

The significant annual decline in labour share that started in 1968 should indicate either a change in technology from labour-using to capital-using technology or an increase in productivity. Figure 6-4, which shows the technological progress function and the non-neutral elasticity of substitution, should give clues about what happened. The technological progress function clearly shows that the change in the industry's technology through time was biased towards labour-using or capital-saving production. But since the value of this function is still less than 1.0, the technology was capital-using, though decreasingly so through time, from 0.57 in 1957 to 0.99 in 1968 and 0.99 in 1977. This then explains, at least in part, the decreasing capital share. The ease with which capital could be substituted by labour is consistent with the technological progress functions. It seems from this variable that these factors of production could have been substituted with greater ease after 1968 than before, although since the value of this variable fluctuated from 0.43 in 1957 to 0.72 in 1977, the production technology was such that substitution would still have been very

49

FIGURE 6-4
ELASTICITY OF SUBSTITUTION AND TECHNOLOGICAL
CHANGE, TEXTILE INDUSTRIES
(in 1971 constant dollars)

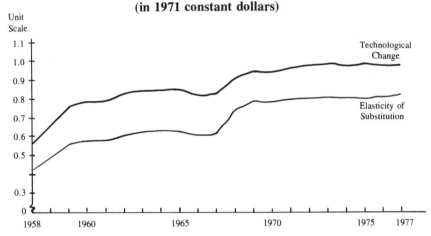

difficult without loss of output and reduced productivity. The regression results of the VES production function show that the average technological advances for the 1957-77 period were 3.4 per cent per annum, which is 0.6 per cent above the sectoral average.

The compounded rate of change in the technological progress function was 1.86 per cent per annum in the 1960s and only 0.59 per cent in the 1970s. This raises another area of investigation — the impact of technological change on labour efficiency. I computed the elasticity of response, m, from the VES production function and found that the value of this impact was 0.19, the lowest in the manufacturing sector. This simply means that the new technology that was introduced in the past had an insignificant impact on labour efficiency. The policy implications are obvious: before any further public aid or loans for technological changes in this industry are granted, a careful study should determine why the new technology had no impact on labour efficiency; as well, the technology that will increase labour efficiency and competitiveness should be determined.

Economies of scale in this industry, according to the Diwan test and the various production functions, did not contribute to growth in labour productivity. In fact, the textile industry experienced diseconomies of scale that grew at a significant rate through time. The importance of economies of scale for productivity is at best questionable for this industry, because labour productivity increased continuously. Overall

50

this industry group has some serious impediments to competing in open markets. But does it have to reach a minimum scale of operation in order to improve its productivity? Or does the problem lie in the quality of plant and equipment? Only a further in-depth study at the industry level could resolve these questions whose answers hold the key to improved competitiveness.

Knitting Mills 7

The knitting mills industry group represents 0.8 per cent of the sectoral value added. It employs 20,700 workers and contains 286 establishments. It ranks twelfth in terms of value added per establishment and employs, on average, 72 workers per establishment. Data for this industry are available in official sources only from 1961.

Capacity Utilization

Figure 7-1 shows the industry potential output plotted against actual value added output, with the gap representing "forgone" output. This figure shows that the industry operated at about 60 per cent of its capacity in 1961, while gradually reaching full capacity utilization in 1973. The industry's capacity utilization fell afterwards to 92 per cent in 1976, recovering to 97 per cent in 1977. A comparison with the sectoral average indicates that prior to 1973 the performance in the industry was inferior to that in the sector, whereas in the post-1973 period the industry outperformed the sector.

Computation of the compounded annual rates of change in capacity utilization shows that the industry increased its utilization rate during the 1960s by 4.35 per cent per year, the highest rate of growth in the manufacturing sector. In the 1970s the industry's capacity utilization increased by 1.53 per cent per year, while the manufacturing sector as a whole showed an annual decrease of 0.34 per cent. In the post-energy crisis era the sector shows a decrease of 2.57 per annum, while the industry experienced a decrease in capacity utilization of 0.73 per cent per year.

Labour Productivity, Capital Intensity, and Real Earnings

An examination of the absolute magnitudes and rates of change of these three variables and their relation to one another may reveal some

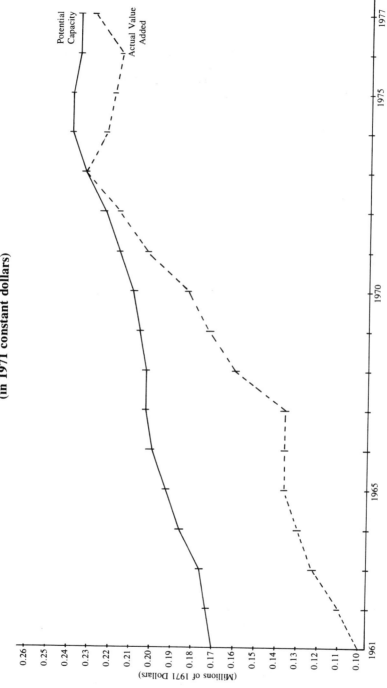

FIGURE 7-1
CAPACITY UTILIZATION, KNITTING MILLS
(in 1971 constant dollars)

53

TABLE 7-1

**AVERAGE ANNUAL PERFORMANCE OF LABOUR PRODUCTIVITY,
CAPITAL INTENSITY, AND REAL EARNINGS,
KNITTING MILLS**

	Knitting Mills	Total Manu.	Industry/ Sector
	(1971 $/hour)		(%)
Labour Productivity			
1946-77		4.93	78.70
1946-60	n.a.	3.50	—
1960-70	2.80	5.34	52.43
1970-77	4.42	7.43	59.49
1973-77	4.70	7.79	60.33
Capital Intensity			
1946-77		5.58	
1946-60	n.a.	4.47	—
1960-70	2.07	6.67	31.03
1970-77	2.73	9.11	29.97
1973-77	2.93	9.53	30.75
Real Earnings			
1946-77	—	2.75	—
1946-60	n.a.	2.07	—
1960-70	1.95	2.96	65.88
1970-77	2.52	3.79	66.49
1973-77	2.66	3.92	67.86

underlying causes for productivity growth in the knitting mills industry. Table 7-1 compares the industry's average performance in these three variables with total manufacturing performance. Average annual labour productivity in the knitting mills industry was significantly lower than that of the sector in every period examined. In fact, during the 1960-70 period average labour productivity in this industry was the lowest in the manufacturing sector. In the 1970-77 period the industry's productivity ranked sixteenth in the sector. Average annual capital intensity in this industry was about 30 per cent of the sector's average in all periods; its capital intensification level placed the industry fifteenth out of the sector's nineteen industry groups. The industry's average real earnings per hour were between 66 and 68 per cent of the sectoral average during all periods.

Figure 7-2 shows more clearly the relative rates of change of these

54

three categories and the constancy of the level of economies of scale throughout the period. The annual rate of change in productivity fluctuated somewhat throughout the seventeen-year period but was clearly greater than the rate of change in real earnings and capital intensity. Specifically, in the 1960s the annual rate of growth in labour productivity in the industry was 6.7 per cent compared with 3.6 per cent in the manufacturing sector. For the same decade, however, real earnings grew by 2.9 per cent per annum, which is similar to the rate in the sector. For the industry it can be said that the rate of growth in real earnings lagged behind that of productivity. In 1970-73 the industry showed a decline in the rates of growth of both productivity and earnings per hour, while in the years after the energy crisis labour productivity increased to 6.3 per cent per year, 4 percentage points above the sectoral rate of growth. Similarly, real earnings per hour showed a considerable annual increase of more than twice the sectoral average.

This kind of information is extremely useful as a guide to labour and management as well as government policy-makers. Industry executives believe that the main reason for the recent lag in labour productivity has been the relatively intensive dose of new technology injected into the production process during the past few years. The industry appears to be undergoing a transformation in its production

FIGURE 7-2
RATES OF CHANGE IN LABOUR PRODUCTIVITY, CAPITAL INTENSITY, REAL EARNINGS, AND ECONOMIES OF SCALE, KNITTING MILLS
(in 1971 constant dollars)

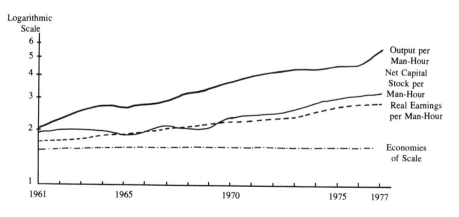

55

processes that will result in increasingly higher productivity per man-hour in years to come.

Similarly, while on average, this industry's capital intensity per man-hour was about one-third of the sectoral level, the rates of growth in Table 7-2 show that the rise in capital intensity accelerated from 2.0 per cent per annum in the 1960s to 5.0 per cent per year in the 1970s, when the rate of growth for the sector was only 3.7 per cent per annum. In the 1970-73 subperiod, we see an annual rate of growth of 6.0 per cent, or three times the sectoral rate, which may have induced the increase in labour productivity in the subsequent subperiod. A note of concern should, however, be recorded, because if the apparent decline in the rate of growth in capital intensity in the 1973-77 subperiod

TABLE 7-2

COMPOUNDED ANNUAL RATES OF CHANGE IN LABOUR PRODUCTIVITY, CAPITAL INTENSITY, AND REAL EARNINGS, KNITTING MILLS

(% in 1971 constant dollars)

	Knitting Mills	Total Manu.	Industry/ Sector
Labour Productivity			
1946-77		3.70	—
1946-60	n.a.	3.82	—
1960-70	6.67	3.64	183.24
1970-77	5.96	3.53	168.84
1970-73	5.51	5.04	109.33
1973-77	6.30	2.41	261.41
Capital Intensity			
1946-77	—	3.83	—
1946-60	n.a.	4.99	—
1960-70	1.99	2.34	85.04
1970-77	4.94	3.66	134.97
1970-73	5.98	1.90	314.7
1973-77	3.57	5.01	71.30
Real Earnings			
1946-77	—	2.85	—
1946-60	n.a.	3.27	—
1960-70	2.88	2.94	97.96
1970-77	3.53	2.31	152.81
1970-73	2.49	2.72	91.54
1973-77	4.32	2.01	214.93

continued, it could slow down the rate of growth in labour productivity in the early 1980s.

Table 7-3 presents four sets of ratios and a measure of the rate of technological change for the industry. The first two deal with the relative relationship between productivity and real earnings. On average, the ratio of labour productivity to real earnings hovered about 80 per cent of that in total manufacturing through three periods. Using annual rates of change rather than absolute magnitudes shows the knitting mills industry lead the sector throughout all periods. Specifically, in the 1960s labour received only 43 per cent of its contribution to change in productivity, and in the 1970s the gains in real earnings were 59 per cent of the gains in labour productivity. Here again we see an example of a potentially misleading notion stemming from average magnitudes: on average, productivity performance in this industry was among the lowest in the sector, but analysis of rates of change places this industry's performance among the top industries in the manufacturing sector.

TABLE 7-3

RATIO OF LABOUR PRODUCTIVITY/EARNINGS, OUTPUT/CAPITAL, AND TECHNOLOGICAL CHANGE, KNITTING MILLS

(in 1971 constant dollars)

	1946-77	1946-60	1960-70	1970-77	1970-73	1973-77
	AVERAGE LABOUR PRODUCTIVITY/AVERAGE REAL EARNINGS					
Total manufacturing	1.79	1.69	1.80	1.96		1.99
Knitting Mills		n.a.	1.44	1.75		1.77
	COMPOUNDED RATES OF CHANGE IN LABOUR PRODUCTIVITY/REAL EARNINGS					
Total manufacturing	1.30	1.17	1.24	1.53	1.85	1.20
Knitting Mills	—	n.a.	2.34	1.69	2.21	1.46
	AVERAGE OUTPUT/AVERAGE CAPITAL					
Total manufacturing	0.81	0.80	0.81	0.82	0.83	0.82
Knitting Mills	—	n.a.	1.53	1.62	1.65	1.65
	COMPOUNDED RATES OF CHANGE IN OUTPUT/CAPITAL					
Total manufacturing	—	—	1.30	−0.16	2.95	−2.43
Knitting Mills	—	n.a.	4.59	0.96	1.83	0.34

	COMPOUNDED RATES OF CHANGE IN TECHNOLOGY (%)		
	1946-77	1960-70	1970-77
Total manufacturing	0.271	0.259	0.361
Knitting Mills	n.a.	−2.562	−1.715

In order to complete the analysis on productivity I traced the productivity of capital — that is, the output-capital ratios — throughout the period. The results in Table 7-3 show the annual average levels of output-capital ratios in the industry to be twice the sectoral average during the 1960s and 1970s. Average capital productivity remained the same — seventh place in the sector — after 1960. But the rates of growth changed the industry's ranking: in the 1960-70 period, the knitting mills industry experienced a 4.6 per cent rate of annual growth in capital productivity, which was the highest in the manufacturing sector; in the 1970-77 period the annual rate of growth declined to less than 1 per cent and the industry's ranking fell back to seventh place in the sector. Nevertheless, growth in output-capital ratios were far superior to those in the sector during the 1970s.

Economies of Scale, Technological Change, Elasticity of Substitution, and Labour Share

Chapter 3 in Volume I revealed that the knitting mills industry experienced diseconomies of scale (0.82) (see Tables 3-4, 3-7). However, a statistical test of the Translog production function shows (Volume I, Table D-4) that the economies of scale variable increased at an insignificantly falling rate. This is also reflected in Figure 7-2, which represents the result of the CES tests, showing almost a constant level of economies of scale through time. The Diwan test also shows that economies of scale did not contribute at all to labour productivity during the 1960-77 period. Yet from the data we see that labour productivity and capital productivity both increased. Thus productivity growth in this industry was not a function of growth in economies of scale.

The rate of change in the technological progress function indicates that the industry consistently used less labour-intensive technology as the period progressed, since a minus sign indicates a decrease in labour-using techniques in production. It progressed from relatively high labour-using technology in 1961 to a "neutral" state in 1977. Figure 7-3 gives an explicit account of the technological progress function, and its relation to the ease with which labour can be substituted by capital. This figure shows a gradual decline in labour-using technology and radically fluctuating elasticity of substitution of the biased type, derived from the VES production function. What this means is that from 1961 to 1968 labour could substitute for capital without reducing the production level of the industry (the values

58

FIGURE 7-3
ELASTICITY OF SUBSTITUTION AND TECHNOLOGICAL
CHANGE, KNITTING MILLS
(in 1971 constant dollars)

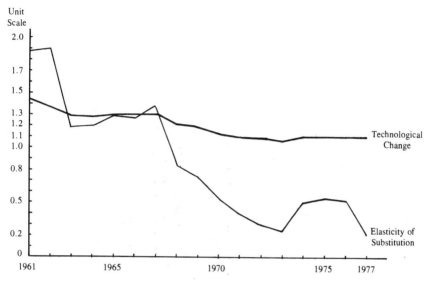

of the variable were 1.89 in 1961 and 1.37 in 1968). After 1968 the value of the elasticity of substitution variable dropped below one, indicating that labour and capital became increasingly dissimilar in the production technology and thus were no longer substitutable for one another. This value dropped from 0.84 in 1968 to 0.22 in 1977, quite unusual behaviour in industries because the elasticity of substitution is generally linked to technological change, which is usually slow.

The only explanation for such fluctuations in the substitution factor is that the industry experienced a finite series of technological "shocks" with extreme changes in 1968 and 1976, rather than a "smooth" gradual transformation throughout. An average measure of the impact of technology on labour efficiency, which is derived from the VES production function (m from Volume I, Table 3-11), shows that in this industry the impact was among the lowest in the sector (0.39). This measure strengthens our assumption of finite shocks towards the tail end of the series. By and large, therefore, the technological changes between 1961 and 1977 were random phenomena rather than planned or continuous changes. Since there is no statistical evidence of a significant impact of new technology on

59

FIGURE 7-4

**RATE OF EARNINGS AND LABOUR SHARE OF VALUE ADDED,
KNITTING MILLS**
(in 1971 constant dollars)

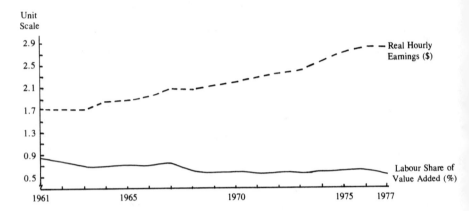

labour productivity, the policy implications are clear: the potential for increased productivity as a result of any government aid — in the form of technological research and development — should be carefully assessed.

Figure 7-4 shows clearly that real hourly earnings in the industry increased through time from $1.72 in 1961 to $2.83 in 1977. Labour's share of value added, however, declined from 83 per cent in 1961 to 51 per cent 1977; by definition, the share of capital was 17 per cent in 1961 and 49 per cent in 1977. Clearly, in spite of increasing real earnings, the knitting mill industry's real hourly earnings were the lowest in the manufacturing sector throughout all periods, and labour received only between 40 and 60 per cent of its contribution to productivity. Two explanations for this low compensation are possible: first, the industry's position in the open market was so tight that its profit structure did not allow a proper reward to labour for its contribution to productivity; or second, management was far more organized than labour and thus dictated the level of wages. In either case the potential exists for increasing productivity by raising the rewards to labour where justifiable on economic grounds.

Clothing Industries

8

The clothing industry group represents 3.3 per cent of the total value added in the manufacturing sector. It employs slightly over 90,000 workers in 2,000 establishments of which 65 per cent are concentrated in Quebec and 23 per cent in Ontario. As a result this analysis bears some regionally specific implications. The industry group ranks twelfth in the number of employees per establishment and seventeenth in value added per establishment. It has faced severe competition from imported clothing — primarily from countries in the Far East — which threatened the survival of many establishments. Presently, a substantial proportion of domestically produced clothing is protected through quotas in order to secure a minimal domestic market. The following analysis assesses part of the impact of the quota policy implemented in 1976 to assist the industry.

Capacity Utilization

Figure 8-1 shows the clothing industry's potential output trend and the industry's actual output since 1946. The clothing industry managed to reach full capacity production only in 1976 (see also Volume I, Tables 3-1 and 3-2). From 1946 to 1960 capacity utilization declined 0.38 per cent per annum; in the 1960s an annual increase of 1.32 per cent prevailed. This increase was slightly above the sectoral average increase for the same decade. In the 1970-77 period, however, the capacity utilization rate accelerated to an annual rate of 3.35 per cent, while total manufacturing experienced a yearly decline of 0.34 per cent. In the 1973-77 subperiod the annual rate of growth in utilization declined to 0.23 per cent, whereas the sectoral rate of change was −2.57 per cent per annum. The industry's performance at 100 per cent of capacity in 1976 and 98 per cent in 1977 could very well be a consequence of the federal government quota policy implemented in 1976. Generally, full capacity operation indicates higher productivity

FIGURE 8-1
CAPACITY UTILIZATION, CLOTHING INDUSTRIES
(in 1971 constant dollars)

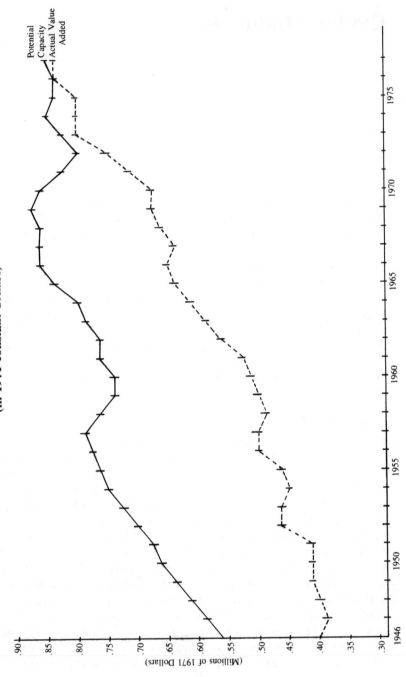

62

or more efficient allocation of factors of production. We proceed now to examine whether the consistency between capacity utilization and productivity prevailed in this industry.

Labour Productivity, Capital Intensity, and Real Earnings

Table 8-1 summarizes the industry's average performance relative to that in the manufacturing sector. Average labour productivity levels in the clothing industry ranged from 57 to 62 per cent of the average sectoral productivity throughout the three decades. In the industry itself, we see an increase of 30 per cent in the level of labour productivity in the 1970s, particularly in the 1973-77 subperiod, which may have contributed to the increase in capacity utilization during the same period. In comparison with the performance of the other eighteen industries in the sector, the clothing industry had the lowest average productivity levels until 1960 (see Volume I, Table 3-18). In the

TABLE 8-1

AVERAGE ANNUAL PERFORMANCE OF LABOUR PRODUCTIVITY, CAPITAL INTENSITY, AND REAL EARNINGS, CLOTHING INDUSTRIES

	Clothing	Total Manu.	Industry/ Sector
	(1971 $/hour)		(%)
Labour Productivity			
1946-77	2.95	4.93	60.0
1946-60	2.12	3.50	61.0
1960-70	3.32	5.34	62.0
1970-77	4.21	7.43	57.0
1973-77	4.44	7.79	57.0
Capital Intensity			
1946-77	0.66	5.58	12.0
1946-60	0.82	4.47	18.0
1960-70	0.76	6.67	11.0
1970-77	0.68	9.11	7.0
1973-77	0.62	9.53	7.0
Real Earnings			
1946-77	2.01	2.75	73.0
1946-60	1.57	2.07	76.0
1960-70	2.10	2.96	71.0
1970-77	2.71	3.79	72.0
1973-77	2.85	3.92	73.0

1960-70 period, it moved to seventeenth place in the sector, retreating to its previous lowest rank in the sector in the 1970s.

The pattern for average capital intensity was similar, with the clothing industry maintaining the lowest rank in the manufacturing sector throughout the whole period. Table 8-1 shows that net capital per man-hour actually declined slightly from 1946 to 1977. Available statistics show us that in the 1950s the average level of capital intensity was 18 per cent of the sectoral average, whereas in the 1970s that figure dropped to 7 per cent. These data simply mean production technology in the clothing industry was primarily labour-intensive and that no significant technological changes occurred during the period.

Average real earnings were consistent with the trend in the other two categories. Table 8-1 shows a gradual increase in average real earnings per hour in this industry, though they remained about 73 per cent of the sectoral average in all periods. The level of real hourly earnings in this industry was the lowest in the manufacturing sector in all the periods examined. This finding is inconsistent with the fact that it was not ranked lowest in average per hour productivity in all the periods. I will refer to this issue below.

Table 8-2 exposes the dynamic changes throughout the thirty-two-year period in the form of compounded annual rates of change of the same variables. It shows that the clothing industry experienced lower annual rates of productivity growth than the sector from 1946 to 1970. In the 1970-77 period, however, the annual rate of growth of labour productivity in this industry exceeded that of the sector by 0.6 percentage points. The strongest annual rate of growth in the industry occurred in the 1973-77 subperiod, exceeding the sectoral rate by almost 2 percentage points. Among the industries in the sector, the industry's growth rate ranked seventeenth from 1946 to 1970 and moved up to tenth in the 1970s.

The rate of growth of capital intensity was somewhat different. In the 1950s the industry's annual rate of growth in capital intensity was half that of the sector. In the 1960s the growth rate in the industry declined and on the average reached only 19 per cent of that of the sector. In the 1970-77 period, however, the annual rate of growth in the industry's capital intensity exceeded that of the sector by 25 per cent. When this subperiod is broken into 1970-73 and 1973-77, we see that capital intensity rose substantially in the first subperiod but its growth rate declined from 7.0 per cent per year in 1970-73 to only 1.5 per cent in 1973-77. The growth rate in the last period was only 29 per cent of the sector's rate of growth. The industry's position in the sector

64

TABLE 8-2

COMPOUNDED ANNUAL RATES OF CHANGE IN LABOUR
PRODUCTIVITY, CAPITAL INTENSITY, REAL EARNINGS AND
AVERAGE PRODUCTIVITY OF CAPITAL, CLOTHING INDUSTRIES

(% in 1971 constant dollars)

	Clothing	Total Manu.	Industry/ Sector
Labour Productivity			
1946-77	3.26	3.70	88.0
1946-60	3.47	3.82	90.8
1960-70	2.38	3.64	65.4
1970-77	4.12	3.53	116.7
1970-73	4.10	5.04	81.3
1973-77	4.14	2.41	171.8
Capital Intensity			
1946-77	1.89	3.83	49.3
1946-60	2.45	4.99	49.1
1960-70	−0.71	2.34	18.9
1970-77	4.57	3.66	124.9
1970-73	6.98	1.90	367.4
1973-77	1.45	5.01	28.8
Real Earnings			
1946-77	2.48	2.85	87.0
1946-60	1.32	3.27	40.4
1960-70	3.42	2.94	116.3
1970-77	3.75	2.31	162.3
1970-73	3.12	2.72	114.7
1973-77	4.23	2.01	210.4
Average Productivity of Capital			
1946-77	—	−0.14	—
1946-60	—	−1.14	—
1960-70	3.18	1.30	244.6
1970-77	−0.38	−0.16	−237.5
1970-73	2.46	2.95	83.4
1973-77	−2.46	−2.43	−101.2

fluctuated considerably as well. In the 1960s it ranked last (nineteenth) in the sector in terms of rates of change in capital intensity, while from 1970 to 1977 it rose to sixth place.

The extreme fluctuation in the range of change in the productivity of capital does not help to explain the industry's pattern of capital intensification. In the 1960s, when the industry ranked the lowest in the rate of growth in capital intensity, Table 8-2 shows the growth in capital productivity to be the highest with over twice the sector's average rate of growth. In the 1970s, when the industry showed an increase in the rate of capital intensification, capital productivity was actually negative. In the 1970-73 subperiod capital productivity rose at about 83 per cent of the sectoral rate of change, but in the 1973-77 subperiod capital productivity declined. The only explanation of this complex pattern is that the new capital invested in this industry did not embody enough new technology to increase productivity. That is, adding capital of similar quality to the old, or simply using the same production technology even with capital replacement, had no positive effect on productivity. Indeed, in the VES function that measures the impact of technology on labour efficiency, the coefficient of m is 0.86, an indication that capital has not been very complementary to labour efficiency in the clothing industry (see Volume I, Table 3-11).

Figure 8-2 shows all these variables discussed so far. From the figure it is easy to see that changes in labour productivity and capital intensity are not consistent. Furthermore, the rates of change in labour productivity and real earnings at times possess different slopes, although they move in the same direction. In addition, as Table 8-3

FIGURE 8-2
RATES OF CHANGE IN LABOUR PRODUCTIVITY, CAPITAL INTENSITY, REAL EARNINGS, AND ECONOMIES OF SCALE, CLOTHING INDUSTRIES
(in 1971 constant dollars)

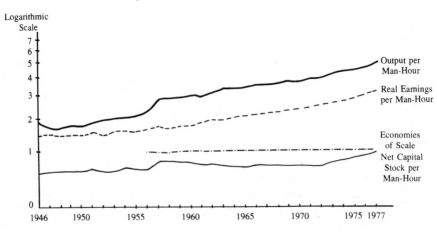

TABLE 8-3

RATIO OF LABOUR PRODUCTIVITY/EARNINGS, OUTPUT/CAPITAL, AND
TECHNOLOGICAL CHANGE,
CLOTHING INDUSTRIES

(in 1971 constant dollars)

	1946-77	1946-60	1960-70	1970-77	1970-73	1973-77
	AVERAGE LABOUR PRODUCTIVITY/AVERAGE REAL EARNINGS					
Total manufacturing	1.79	1.69	1.80	1.96		1.99
Clothing	1.47	1.35	1.58	1.55		1.56
	COMPOUNDED RATES OF CHANGE IN LABOUR PRODUCTIVITY/REAL EARNINGS					
Total manufacturing	1.30	1.17	1.24	1.53	1.85	1.20
Clothing	1.32	2.63	1.27	1.10	1.31	0.98
	AVERAGE OUTPUT/AVERAGE CAPITAL					
Total manufacturing	0.81	0.80	0.81	0.82	0.83	0.82
Clothing	—	—	4.43	5.55	5.72	5.47
	COMPOUNDED RATES OF CHANGE IN OUTPUT/CAPITAL					
Total manufacturing	−0.14	−1.14	1.30	−0.16	2.95	−2.43
Clothing	—	—	3.18	−0.38	2.46	−2.46

	COMPOUNDED RATES OF CHANGE IN TECHNOLOGY (%)		
	1946-77	1960-70	1970-77
Total manufacturing	0.271	0.259	0.361
Clothing	0.137	0.636	−0.380

shows, the ratio of the rate of change in labour productivity to the rate
of change in real earnings was greater than one from 1946 to 1973 and
above the sector ratio up to 1970, which means that annual increases in
labour productivity were greater than increases in real earnings in this
industry for twenty-five years. However, during the 1970-77 period
labour received its marginal product in real earnings (1.10).

Technological Change, Elasticity of Substitution, Labour Share, and Economies of Scale

In general, technological progress and capital productivity are
expected to be related in a consistent manner. In this industry,
however, that is not the case. Table 8-2 shows an increase in average
productivity of capital in the 1960s of 3.18 per cent per year. The
technological progress variable of the VES production function shows
that during that period the trend was towards a labour-using rather than
a capital-using production technology. At the other extreme, in

FIGURE 8-3
ELASTICITY OF SUBSTITUTION AND TECHNOLOGICAL
CHANGE, CLOTHING INDUSTRIES
(in 1971 constant dollars)

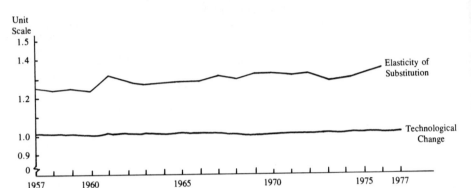

1970-77, the average productivity of capital was negative, while the technological progress function indicated a tendency towards capital-using technology during the same period. From the regression results in Table D-3 in Volume I, we see that, on average, for the 1957-77 period productivity growth attributable to technological gains was 1.2 per cent in the industry versus 2.9 per cent in the sector. In addition, Figure 8-3 shows that production technology was almost constant after 1957, while the elasticity of substitution was constantly above one and increasing. The conclusion to be drawn is that with existing production technology in this industry, capital investments were redundant and did not advance productivity growth.

Figure 8-4 shows the pattern of real earnings per hour and of labour share of value added. Real earnings increased steadily in this industry, with a relatively higher annual increase after 1974. Although hourly earnings were among the lowest in the sector, within the industry and with respect to its changing productivity rates, the pattern of hourly earnings seems rational after 1970, when labour began to receive roughly its marginal product in recent years. The labour share of value added increased slightly between 1957 and 1976 and dropped slightly in 1977. This is consistent with the technological progress function, which changed little throughout this period. The decline in 1977 reflects the larger payment to capital, which was also indicated in the pattern of change of technological progress towards a higher level of capital-using technology (Figure 8-3).

68

FIGURE 8-4
RATE OF EARNINGS AND LABOUR SHARE OF VALUE ADDED, CLOTHING INDUSTRIES
(in 1971 constant dollars)

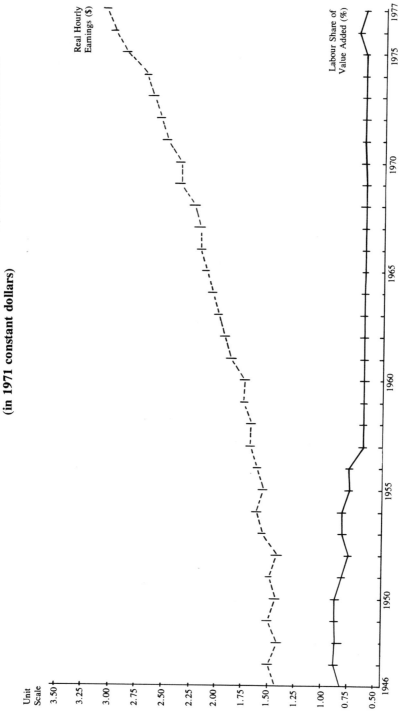

In conclusion, although it is too early to assess the results of the government quota restrictions to assist the clothing industry, early trends show rising capacity utilization and labour productivity. Increases in capital intensity did not significantly raise labour productivity basically because this is a labour-intensive industry with insignificant technological advances. Although quota controls may prove highly beneficial for the industry, they are punitive to consumers because such protective measures are another form of indirect tax on consumers who are thereby subsidizing marginal producers. Therefore, such measures should always be of a short-term nature.

The industry enjoyed slight economies of scale throughout the period 1957-77, starting with 0.99 in 1957 and increasing to 1.04 in 1977 (see Figure 8-2 and Volume I, Table 3-4). The Translog function gave similar trend results but slightly greater economies of scale (1.24 in Volume I, Table D-4) growing at an increasing rate (Volume I, Table 3-6). If the constraints on increasing productivity are lack of scale economies and product diversity, then longer runs of fewer products are likely to increase productivity. Indications of recent scale increases are promising for this industry. So far, however, the Diwan test shows that economies of scale have not contributed at all to labour productivity (see Volume I, Table 3-10).

Wood Industries 9

The wood industries group represents 5.7 per cent of total manufacturing value added. It employs 90,000 people in 2,700 establishments, with an average of 33 employees each, and ranks sixteenth in terms of value added per establishment.

Capacity Utilization

Figure 9-1 shows the industries' potential capacity output, which indicates the level of output that could be obtained had they utilized the total production resources at their direct command. This figure also shows the industries' actual value added in each year since 1957. The difference between these two indicates the unutilized capacity through time, and thus the output forgone. The industry group operated rather close to full capacity between 1957 and 1964 when it reached full capacity. The utilization rate then dropped gradually to 80 per cent in 1970, climbed again to 85 per cent in 1973, and declined to a low point of 66 per cent in 1975 (see Volume I, Table 3-1). This pattern of fluctuation yielded a V-shaped diagram from 1957 to 1975. Between 1975 and 1977, however, the industry group recovered 15 per cent in capacity utilization and ended up utilizing 80 per cent of its production capacity in 1977. A comparison of the industry group with total manufacturing shows that in the 1960-70 period the sector increased its capacity utilization by an annual rate of 1.15 per cent, while the wood industries capacity utilization rate decreased by 1.33 per cent per year for the same period. In the 1970-77 period, capacity utilization decreased in the manufacturing sector by 0.34 per cent per annum, while this industry group increased its rate by 0.05 per cent per year. After the energy crisis (1973-77), however, the sector's capacity utilization rate showed an annual decline of 2.57 per cent, whereas the wood industries' annual rate of decrease was 1.53 per cent. However,

FIGURE 9-1
CAPACITY UTILIZATION, WOOD INDUSTRIES
(in 1971 constant dollars)

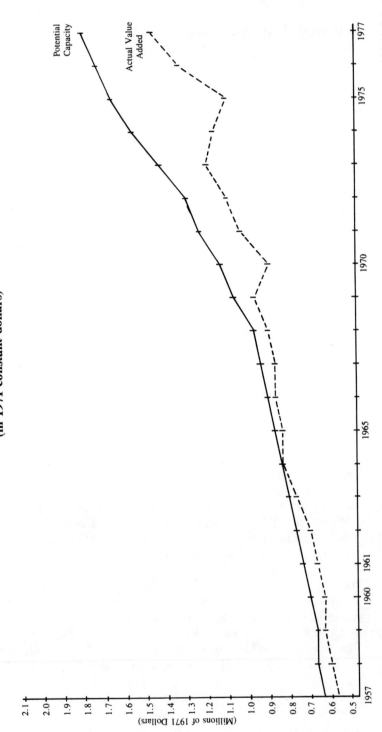

examination of the annual utilization figures (see Volume I, Table 3-1), reflected in Figure 9-1, demonstrates that the industries *increased* their capacity utilization from 74.9 per cent in 1974 to 80.3 per cent in 1977, indicating that the energy crisis had no deleterious effect on the wood industries' capacity utilization.

Labour Productivity, Capital Intensity, and Real Earnings

Table 9-1 compares the wood industries' average performance in three variables with that in total manufacturing. Average labour productivity in the wood industries was 18 per cent below the sectoral average in the 1960s and 24 per cent below it in the 1970s. But in the 1973-77 subperiod they outperformed the sectoral average by 20 per cent. Average industrial levels of capital intensity were consistently below the sectoral average after 1960. Average productivity levels of both variables rose 29 per cent from the 1960s to the 1970s, while the

TABLE 9-1

AVERAGE ANNUAL PERFORMANCE OF LABOUR PRODUCTIVITY, CAPITAL INTENSITY, AND REAL EARNINGS, WOOD INDUSTRIES

	Wood	Total Manu.	Industry/ Sector
	(1971 $/hour)		(%)
Labour Productivity			
1946-77	3.63	4.93	74.0
1946-60	2.17	3.50	62.0
1960-70	4.39	5.34	82.0
1970-77	5.68	7.43	76.0
1973-77	5.92	4.93	120.0
Capital Intensity			
1946-77	3.87	5.58	69.4
1946-60	2.10	4.47	47.0
1960-70	4.27	6.67	64.0
1970-77	7.07	9.11	77.6
1973-77	7.76	9.53	81.4
Real Earnings			
1946-77	2.45	2.75	89.1
1946-60	1.63	2.07	78.7
1960-70	2.61	2.96	88.2
1970-77	3.82	3.79	100.8
1973-77	4.09	3.92	104.3

73

increase in the level of capital intensity was 65 per cent for the same period. Capital intensification thus outstripped labour productivity almost threefold. But unless a very long lag between capital investment and increased productivity is typical in this industry group, the line between capital intensification and rising labour productivity can hardly be established. On the basis of labour productivity, the wood industries group ranked fourteenth in the sector during the 1960s and 1970s, and on the basis of capital intensity, it was twelfth in the 1960s and tenth in the 1970s.

The progression of average real earnings is also shown in this table. In the 1960-70 period real earnings per hour were about 88 per cent of the average level in the sector, while in 1970-77 the levels of the wood industries and the sector were similar. One fact should, however, be kept in mind for later comparison; that is, the increase in real earnings from the 1960s to the 1970s was 46 per cent, while the average productivity increase between the same periods was only 29 per cent. For further insight into the rates of growth of these three variables we turn to Table 9-2 and Figure 9-2. Although data are available from 1946 on, there was a severe inconsistency between the 1946-57 and 1957-77 subseries; for example, see the ''jump'' in productivity and capital intensity in 1956-57 in Figure 9-2. The quality of data up to 1957 was questioned and thus all econometric tests were conducted for 1957-77 only.

Table 9-2 shows that the annual rate of growth in labour productivity

FIGURE 9-2
RATES OF CHANGE IN LABOUR PRODUCTIVITY, CAPITAL INTENSITY, REAL EARNINGS, AND ECONOMIES OF SCALE, WOOD INDUSTRIES
(in 1971 constant dollars)

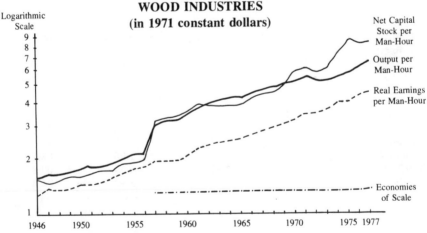

in the wood industries was above that of the sector in the three major periods. When the 1970-77 period was divided into two shorter subperiods it appeared that from 1970 to 1973 there was a significant drop in the annual rate of growth of labour productivity in this industry group, to only 20 per cent of the sectoral rate of change. In 1973-77, however, labour productivity in the industries "jumped" sixfold to 2.5 times the sectoral rate of annual growth. Note, however, that because of the shortness of these two subperiods the random errors could be large and a portion of these severe fluctuations could represent "noise" in the series. Nonetheless, unquestionably productivity in the wood industries was much higher after the energy crisis than before it.

The relative position of the industry group in the sector fluctuated radically in terms of the annual rates of change in labour productivity. In the 1950s this group of industries was eighth in the sector, in the

TABLE 9-2

COMPOUNDED ANNUAL RATES OF CHANGE IN LABOUR PRODUCTIVITY, CAPITAL INTENSITY, AND REAL EARNINGS, WOOD INDUSTRIES

(% in 1971 constant dollars)

	Wood	Total Manu.	Industry/ Sector
Labour Productivity			
1946-77	4.88	3.70	131.9
1946-60	5.99	3.82	156.8
1960-70	4.00	3.64	109.9
1970-77	3.94	3.53	111.6
1970-73	1.02	5.04	20.2
1973-77	6.19	2.41	256.8
Capital Intensity			
1946-77	5.66	3.83	147.8
1946-60	6.20	4.99	124.2
1960-70	5.18	2.34	221.4
1970-77	5.28	3.66	144.3
1970-73	8.65	1.90	455.3
1973-77	0.95	5.01	19.0
Real Earnings			
1946-77	4.15	2.85	145.6
1946-60	3.46	3.27	105.8
1960-70	4.54	2.94	154.4
1970-77	5.01	2.31	216.9
1970-73	4.47	2.72	164.3
1973-77	5.42	2.01	269.7

1960s it advanced to fourth place, and in the 1970s it retreated to twelfth place. In the 1970-73 subperiod these industries experienced the lowest annual rate of change in labour productivity, while in 1973-77 their performance was in fourth place out of nineteen industry groups.

The annual rates of growth in capital intensity were consistent with those of labour productivity up to 1969, when the rates of change in capital intensity exceeded considerably those of productivity (see Figure 9-2). Table 9-2 also discloses that throughout the whole period the industries' rate of growth in capital intensity was far higher than the sector's, except during the 1973-77 subperiod. In the 1960s the industries' annual rate of capital intensification was the fastest in the sector, whereas in the 1970s it was the fourth.

Real earnings grew steadily at increasing annual rates, which were always above the sector's rates of change. Table 9-2 and Figure 9-2 indicate that the annual rate of growth in real earnings exceeded that of labour productivity.

Table 9-3 shows the relationship between labour productivity and real wages and output-capital ratios. Annual averages of the ratios of productivity to earning were 1.7 in the 1960s and 1.5 in the 1970s; on average, therefore, the level of labour productivity was 68 per cent and 50 per cent higher than the level of real earnings during these periods, respectively. In both periods the industries' average level was lower than that of the sector.

But averages, as emphasized throughout the study, do not bear serious policy implications because they do not reflect the dynamic changes in the industry. The compounded annual rate of growth of the same ratio reflects the productivity performance within the industries relative to their payments to labour (in real terms), and includes the impact of external factors on them such as market forces and market structure.

In the 1950s the wood industries experienced a unique situation when the ratio of productivity growth to that of earnings assumed an annual rate of change of 1.7, compared with 1.2 in the sector. This implies an annual rate of net gain in productivity of 70 per cent. From the labour point of view that situation was far less than desirable, for the rate of increase of its productivity was 70 per cent beyond what it received in real earnings. From the 1960s on the situation reversed. In the 1960s labour received an annual increase in real earnings of 1.14 beyond its contribution to the rate of growth in productivity. The industry "overpaid" labour beyond its change in income from

76

TABLE 9-3

RATIO OF LABOUR PRODUCTIVITY/EARNINGS, OUTPUT/CAPITAL, AND TECHNOLOGICAL CHANGE, WOOD INDUSTRIES

(in 1971 constant dollars)

	1946-77	1946-60	1960-70	1970-77	1970-73	1973-77
	AVERAGE LABOUR PRODUCTIVITY/AVERAGE REAL EARNINGS					
Total manufacturing	1.79	1.69	1.80	1.96		1.99
Wood	1.48	1.33	1.68	1.49		1.45
	COMPOUNDED RATES OF CHANGE IN LABOUR PRODUCTIVITY/REAL EARNINGS					
Total manufacturing	1.30	1.17	1.24	1.53	1.85	1.20
Wood	1.18	1.73	0.88	0.79	0.23	1.14
	AVERAGE OUTPUT/AVERAGE CAPITAL					
Total manufacturing	0.81	0.80	0.81	0.82	0.83	0.82
Wood	—	n.a.	1.04	0.82	0.89	0.77
	COMPOUNDED RATES OF CHANGE IN OUTPUT/CAPITAL					
Total manufacturing	−0.14	−1.14	1.30	−0.16	2.95	−2.43
Wood	—	n.a.	−1.12	−1.28	0.0	−2.23
	COMPOUNDED RATES OF CHANGE IN TECHNOLOGY (%)					
	1946-77	1960-70	1970-77			
Total manufacturing	0.271	0.259	0.361			
Wood	−0.306	−0.459	−1.206			

production. In the 1970s this situation was exacerbated, when the rate of change in labour earnings was 27 per cent greater than the rate of change in its productivity. In the 1970-73 subperiod annual increases in real earnings in the wood industries were 4.3 times higher than the rate of change in labour productivity; that is, labour produced only 23 per cent of its real earnings increases. In 1973-77 this unhealthy situation came to an end and labour received roughly its contribution to increased productivity.

When labour is compensated at a higher rate than that at which it produces one of two structures is likely to be created: the industry will constantly have to absorb the penalty of excess payments to labour by decreasing its profitability position; or the industry will have to set higher prices for its products in order to recover the excess payments to labour. The first would have occurred if consumers of the wood industries' products had many satisfactory substitutes for wood products, for as wood products' prices increased, consumers would have turned to these substitutes and either ceased to purchase wood products or decreased their consumption more than proportionately to the price increases. This situation is generally defined as relatively high price elasticity of demand for products. The second case would have occurred if there were few or virtually no substitutes for the industries' products. In this instance, consumers would have very little or no choice and, regardless of price increases, they would continue to consume the products in question. Such a situation is described as relatively low price elasticity of (or inelastic) demand. When an industry is in such a state, the increase in prices is by and large transferred to consumers, a phenomenon that tends to be inflationary. The other extreme could occur when an industry, because of its size and resource control, dictates market prices. The wood industries fell somewhere between the two during the period examined; that is, some losses were absorbed by the industries and some price increases were absorbed by customers.

Since the pure principles of comparative advantage do not hold nowadays for intercounty commodity flows, outside intervention is necessary to help an industry "normalize" its operation for the sake of price stability. This particular industry group indirectly affects the level of prices in many related industries, such as construction, and thus it is desirable to trace the source of its productivity setbacks, which brings us to an examination of the productivity of capital and the impact of new technology on labour efficiency. Table 9-3 provides some insights into the question of capital productivity, indicating that after 1960 there was a consistent and increasing negative annual rate of change in the output-capital ratio. This simply means that the rate of productivity of capital was *negative* and increasingly so, one of the major constraints on productivity increases in this industry group.

Evidence from our estimates of the VES production function shows that total productivity growth attributable to technological improvement in this industry group during the 1957-77 period was 1.5 per cent compared with the sectoral average of 2.9 per cent (Volume I, Table D-3). The industries appear to have experienced a regression of the quality in their capital — some would say obsolescence of plant and equipment — rather than "shocks" of new technology.

The strategic question is how the industries would respond to new technology embodied in their changing stock of capital. One answer stems from the results obtained from the m parameter in the VES function. The value of m, which represents the elasticity of response to the introduction of new technology, is 1.59 for the wood industries (Volume I, Table 3-11), the fourth largest in the manufacturing sector.

Thus an increase of 1.59 per cent in labour efficiency would result from a 1 per cent rise in new technology, and a deterioration of technology through depletion of capital stock would have a significant impact on labour efficiency.

Technological Change, Elasticity of Substitution, Labour Share, and Economies of Scale

The technological progress variable provides information on the type of technology used by the firm or industry in its production process. If it is greater than one, technology tends to be labour using; if it is less than one, capital-using technology is implied. Table 9-3 indicates that the technical rate of change tended to be capital using after 1960 and increasingly so after 1970. Figure 9-3 displays in finer detail the industries' technical progress since 1957, showing that their technology has all along been capital using or labour saving, since the function fluctuates between 0.72 and 0.84. But changes began in 1971. From 1971 to 1975 the industry increased its capital-using technology by 4.06 per cent per year, while from 1975 to 1977 it increased its labour-using technology by 4.7 per cent yearly. Since g was below one during the whole period, the changes in the value of g do not imply a radical change in technology from capital-intensive to labour-intensive methods; rather changes were tending towards labour-saving or -using technologies while remaining within the general range of capital-using technology.

The ease with which factors of production can be substituted for one another without reducing total production is estimated by using a production function to calculate elasticity of substitution. Here these results come from the VES production function, because its form allows the elasticity of substitution to vary over time. This variable is plotted in Figure 9-3 and is consistent with the technical progress variable. Its value in 1957 was 0.62 and fluctuated similarly to g up to 1974, reaching a value of 0.54 in that year. From 1974 to 1977 it increased by 3 per cent per year to a level of 0.59. When the value of the elasticity of substitution variable is less than one, factors of production are dissimilar and hence are not easily substituted without jeopardising total productivity levels. Usually, industries that use capital-intensive technology possess low substitutability, and the wood industries seem to belong to such a category.

Figure 9-4 shows the pattern of change in real earnings and that of the labour share of value added output. The labour share remained relatively constant from 1958 to 1970 at about 0.60 or 60 per cent of

FIGURE 9-3
ELASTICITY OF SUBSTITUTION AND TECHNOLOGICAL CHANGE, WOOD INDUSTRIES
(in 1971 constant dollars)

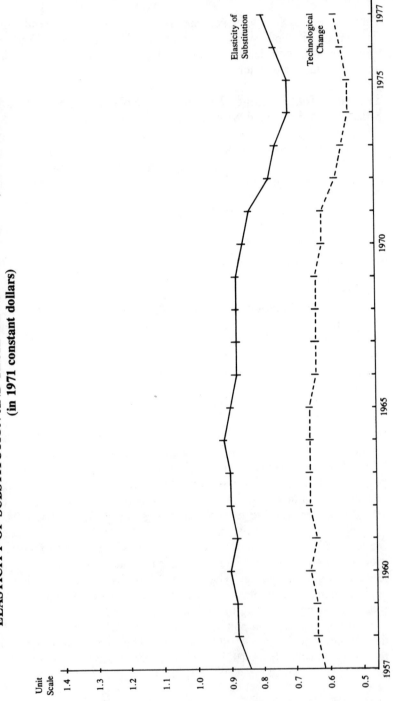

FIGURE 9-4
RATE OF EARNINGS AND LABOUR SHARE OF VALUE ADDED, WOOD INDUSTRIES
(in 1971 constant dollars)

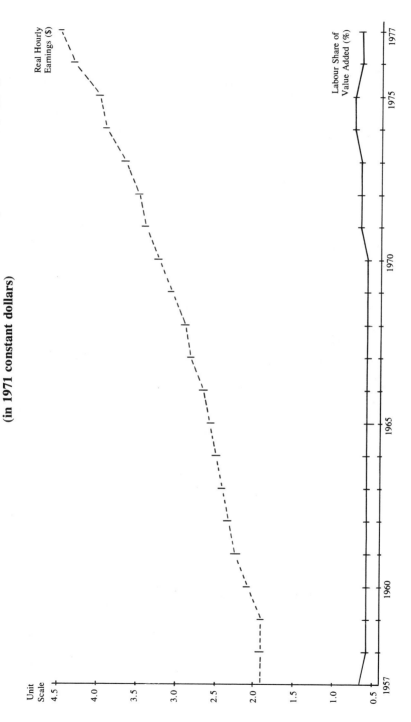

value added; during that period payment to capital was around 40 per cent of value added output. Real earnings during that period increased from $1.92 in 1958 to $3.21 in 1970, or by 4.4 per cent per annum (compounded). Between 1970 and 1975 the share of labour increased from 0.62 to 0.71, or 2.8 per cent per year (compounded). From 1975 to 1977 the labour share declined by 2.9 per cent per year, while real earnings increased by 6.3 per cent. This supports our earlier discussion where the rates of change in capital intensity and productivity were quite similar to the increased rate in real earnings for the same period. Conversely, in the 1970-73 subperiod real wages increased at a far faster pace than productivity, while the increase in the rate of capital intensity did not rise as far as the productivity of capital.

The relationship, or the lack of one, between productivity performance and economies of scale is especially important for policy decisions affecting the wood industries. Economies of scale ranged from 1.32 to 1.35 in the 1957-77 period, using the three production functions (Volume I, Table 3-3); that is, a 1 per cent increase in factor inputs yielded 1.35 per cent more output. The specific pattern of economies of scale through time is important, because 1.35 is a static average for the period that might have increased or decreased at certain times. The Translog production function shows that economies of scale grew at a *declining rate* though in a statistically insignificant way (see Tables 3-6 and D-4 in Volume I). Thus through time, the increase in inputs gave smaller gains in output, but not by much less than the 1.35 average. The Diwan test identified the contributions of economies of scale to growth in labour productivity as 6 per cent, compared with the sectoral average of 31 per cent, ranking the wood industries tenth in terms of this variable. There is, therefore, no clearcut relationship in this industry between economies of scale and productivity growth rates. It was in seventh place in terms of economies of scale, but in terms of marginal productivity it fluctuated from fourth place in the 1960s to twelfth place in the 1970s. In terms of average productivity, it maintained a stable fourteenth place in the sector.

These industries are among the "natural" ones for the Canadian economy, since they have a large resource endowment and thus a comparative advantage. To become internationally competitive the productivity of capital — the weakest feature of the industries — must be raised. Only through an in-depth study of the industries' present problems and their ability to absorb new technology through high-quality capital can capital productivity be achieved. Such a study should be required by federal and provincial governments before they make any further long-term loans or grants to these industries.

82

Furniture and Fixtures Industries

10

This industry group represents 2 per cent of total manufacturing value added, employs 40,000 people in 1,752 establishments, giving it the lowest value added output per establishment in this sector. On average each establishment employs 23 workers.

Capacity Utilization

Figure 10-1 shows the industry's potential capacity output had the industry utilized all the production resources under its direct command, and the industry's actual value added output during the 1961-77 period. The gap between these two curves shows the unutilized potential output and thus the income that could have been earned had the industry utilized its full production potential. The furniture and fixtures industries reached their full capacity utilization in 1966, after a gradual increase from 75 per cent in 1961. After 1966 utilization rates fluctuated somewhat, declining to a low of 80 per cent in 1971 and rising to a high of 91 per cent in 1973. From 1973 on the capacity utilization rates fell continually, reaching a low of 76 per cent in 1977. Unlike several of the other industries, this group operated at full capacity only in 1966; in all other years it experienced varying degrees of excess capacity.

The industry's annual rate of change in capacity utilization in the 1960-70 period was 0.85 per cent compared with 1.15 per cent in the sector. In the 1970-77 period it experienced an annual rate of decline of 0.87 per cent, while the sector's rate of decline was 0.34 per cent. In the 1973-77 subperiod, its rate of decline was 4.46 per cent per year, while the sector's was 2.57 per cent per annum. In the 1960s and early 1970s the industry's annual rate of growth in utilization ranked thirteenth in the sector. After 1973, however, the industry group's rate of annual decline was its own worst in seventeen years and the third largest in the sector. The figure shows the largest decline in capacity

FIGURE 10-1
CAPACITY UTILIZATION, FURNITURE AND FIXTURES INDUSTRIES
(in 1971 constant dollars)

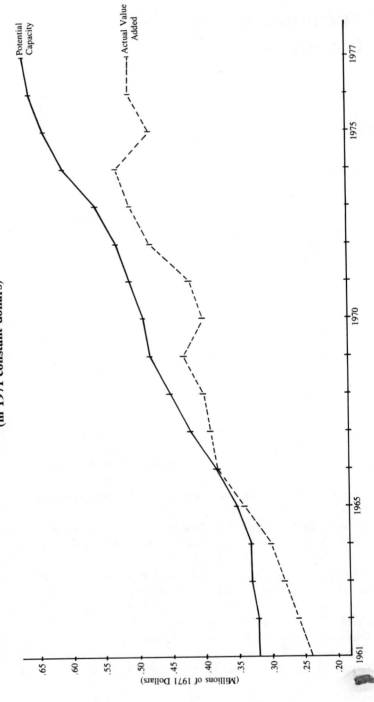

utilization between 1973 and 1975 with a slight recuperation in 1976-77. This setback in capacity utilization could have been caused by a combination of factors on the supply side, such as price increases as a result of the energy crisis, and on the demand side, such as the 1975 recession in domestic and U.S. markets.

Since this industry group has the smallest number of employees and the smallest value added per establishment in the sector, I tend to accept weakening demand conditions as a dominant factor in that slowdown. The industry is not concentrated enough to exert power over market prices, the products are highly differentiated, and a large number of substitutes (such as imports) with considerable price variability exist in the market. These, and the fact that a replacement of furniture can be "postponed" in hard economic times, imply relatively high price and income elasticities of demand for these products and that recession would severely affect this industry.

Labour Productivity, Capital Intensity, and Real Earnings

Table 10-1 compares the industry's annual average performance in terms of these three variables with that in total manufacturing. Average labour productivity was below the sector average by over 30 per cent throughout all periods. Within the sector this industry group ranked sixteenth during the 1960s and seventeenth during the 1970s, or fourth and third lowest respectively in average annual productivity levels. The average level of capital intensity in the group was only 22 to 25 per cent of the sector average in all periods, placing it seventeenth throughout the period. The average level of real earnings per hour was about 80 per cent of that in total manufacturing from 1960 to 1977. Relative to other industries in the sector, this industry group maintained the sixteenth place in both decades.

The compounded annual rates of change in these variables demonstrated more encouraging trends (Table 10-2 and Figure 10-2). Labour productivity displayed a continuous rate of increase in the industry through the 1960s and 1970s, including the post-energy crisis years. In fact, this industry experienced a slight annual decrease in the annual rate of growth in labour productivity from 1970 to 1973 but a rise of 0.5 percentage points in annual growth from 1973 to 1977. Comparing the industry's pattern of productivity growth with total manufacturing revealed that in the 1960s the annual rates of growth were similar in both. But in the 1970s the industry group experienced a slight annual rise in its rate of growth, while the sector experienced a slight decline. In the 1970-73 subperiod, the sector's rate of growth

TABLE 10-1

AVERAGE ANNUAL PERFORMANCE OF LABOUR PRODUCTIVITY, CAPITAL INTENSITY, AND REAL EARNINGS, FURNITURE AND FIXTURES INDUSTRIES

	Furniture and Fixtures	Total Manu.	Industry/ Sector
	(1971 $/hour)		(%)
Labour Productivity			
1946-77	—	4.93	—
1946-60	n.a.	3.50	—
1960-70	3.89	5.34	72.8
1970-77	4.91	7.43	66.1
1973-77	5.13	7.79	65.9
Capital Intensity			
1946-77	—	5.58	—
1946-60	n.a.	4.47	—
1960-70	1.45	6.67	21.7
1970-77	2.22	9.11	24.4
1973-77	2.35	9.53	24.7
Real Earnings			
1946-77	—	2.75	—
1946-60	n.a.	2.07	—
1960-70	2.37	2.96	80.3
1970-77	2.98	3.79	78.6
1973-77	3.11	3.92	79.3

FIGURE 10-2

RATES OF CHANGE IN LABOUR PRODUCTIVITY, CAPITAL INTENSITY, REAL EARNINGS, AND ECONOMIES OF SCALE, FURNITURE AND FIXTURES INDUSTRIES
(in 1971 constant dollars)

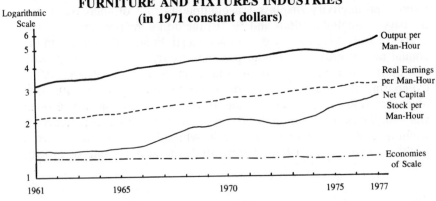

increased by 1.5 percentage points (from 3.53 to 5.04 per cent), whereas the furniture industry experienced a slight decline to 3.4 per cent per year. Between 1973 and 1977 total manufacturing showed a significant decline in productivity growth from 5.04 to 2.4 per cent per year, while the industry's growth rate increased from 3.4 to 3.9 per cent per year — another example where the aggregate analysis does not necessarily hold for the elements contained it it.

The industry's standing within the sector fluctuated. The rate of growth in productivity in the 1960s placed it ninth and in the 1970s, thirteenth. In the 1970-73 subperiod it had the lowest rate of productivity growth in the sector, whereas in 1973-77 it advanced to tenth place. The annual rate of growth in real earnings in the industry group was much slower than that of labour productivity, but roughly equivalent to the rate of growth of total manufacturing. Within the sector, however, the industry ranked sixteenth in the 1960s and 1970s in the level of average real earnings and twelfth in rates of growth of earnings. Figure 10-2 demonstrates clearly the relationship between changes in productivity and real earnings; it shows that the slope of productivity is steeper than that of real earnings particularly from 1975 on.

The rate of growth in capital intensity is the last category in this table. In the 1960s the annual rate of growth was almost twice the sectoral rate, while in the 1970s it was greater than the sector's by 11 per cent. Figure 10-2 illustrates the fluctuations in capital intensity in greater detail and reveals that most of the growth in the 1960s really occurred from 1966 to 1970, then a decline in the rate of growth dominated the series until 1972 when the industry began to experience an unprecedented high rate of growth in capital intensity (8.13 per cent per annum). The rates of growth in productivity and capital intensity were inconsistent from 1966 to 1975 (Figure 10-2). Clearly, from 1966 to 1971 the rate of growth in capital intensity had no direct impact on the rate of growth in labour productivity. Only from 1975 until 1977 were these two variables consistent with each other. Within the sector, the furniture industry's annual rate of growth of capital intensity was the highest in the sector in the 1960s, whereas in the 1970s it retreated to fourth place.

Table 10-3, which examines the relationship between labour productivity and real earnings and capital productivity, reveals that on the average, the ratio of labour productivity to real returns to labour was 1.64 for the industry, or about 10 per cent below the sector average. This means that on average labour received 61 per cent of its contribution to productivity growth.

TABLE 10-2

COMPOUNDED ANNUAL RATES OF CHANGE IN LABOUR PRODUCTIVITY, CAPITAL INTENSITY, AND REAL EARNINGS, FURNITURE AND FIXTURES INDUSTRIES

(% in 1971 constant dollars)

	Furniture and Fixtures	Total Manu.	Industry/ Sector
Labour Productivity			
1946-77	—	3.70	—
1946-60	n.a.	3.82	—
1960-70	3.56	3.64	97.8
1970-77	3.68	3.53	104.2
1970-73	3.38	5.04	67.1
1973-77	3.91	2.41	162.2
Capital Intensity			
1946-77	—	3.83	—
1946-60	n.a.	4.99	—
1960-70	4.30	2.34	183.8
1970-77	4.05	3.66	110.7
1970-73	−1.15	1.90	22.0
1973-77	8.13	5.01	162.3
Real Earnings			
1946-77	—	2.85	—
1946-60	n.a.	3.27	—
1960-70	2.86	2.94	97.3
1970-77	2.71	2.31	117.3
1970-73	2.39	2.72	87.9
1973-77	2.95	2.01	146.8

Since averages may be misleading for policy considerations, we turn to the compounded rates of annual change of the same ratio, which show that during the 1960-70 period the annual increase in real earnings was 80 per cent of labour contribution to productivity growth, while in 1970-77 it dropped to 74 per cent. Average figures show that capital productivity throughout was very high, at about three times the sectoral average. The contribution of capital to the productivity growth was negative in both decades and inferior to that of the sector. An exception occurred during the pre-energy crisis years, when the rate of change in the productivity of capital was extremely high (4.5 per cent

88

TABLE 10-3

RATIO OF LABOUR PRODUCTIVITY/EARNINGS, OUTPUT/CAPITAL, AND
TECHNOLOGICAL CHANGE,
FURNITURE AND FIXTURES INDUSTRIES

(in 1971 constant dollars)

	1946-77	1946-60	1960-70	1970-77	1970-73	1973-77
	AVERAGE LABOUR PRODUCTIVITY/AVERAGE REAL EARNINGS					
Total manufacturing	1.79	1.69	1.80	1.96		1.99
Furniture and Fixtures	—	n.a.	1.64	1.65		1.65
	COMPOUNDED RATES OF CHANGE IN LABOUR PRODUCTIVITY/REAL EARNINGS					
Total manufacturing	1.30	1.17	1.24	1.53	1.85	1.20
Furniture and Fixtures	—	n.a.	1.25	1.36	1.41	1.33
	AVERAGE OUTPUT/AVERAGE CAPITAL					
Total manufacturing	0.81	0.80	0.81	0.82	0.83	0.82
Furniture and Fixtures	—	n.a.	2.46	2.23	2.33	2.20
	COMPOUNDED RATES OF CHANGE IN OUTPUT/CAPITAL					
Total manufacturing	−0.14	−1.14	1.30	−0.16	2.95	−2.43
Furniture and Fixtures	—	n.a.	−0.70	−0.40	4.50	−3.92
	COMPOUNDED RATES OF CHANGE IN TECHNOLOGY (%)					
	1946-77	1960-70	1970-77			
Total manufacturing	0.271	0.259	0.361			
Furniture and Fixtures	0.264	0.237	0.289			

per year) in spite of a negative rate (−1.15 per cent per year) of growth in capital intensity during these three years (see Table 10-2). In 1973-77 capital intensity grew at an annual rate of 8.13 per cent, while capital productivity declined at a rate of 3.92 per cent per year. Low capital productivity has, therefore, been a problem for this industry and has severely constrained further total productivity growth. The question then is whether it is the quality of capital that caused the problem in the industry, or its inability to absorb capital and convert it to a highly productive factor of production.

The answer may be found in the measure of the impact of technology (assuming that capital introduces technology) on labour efficiency. Results from our VES production function show that the impact of technology on labour efficiency during the past two decades was only 1.08 (see Volume I, Table 3-11) — signifying that the productivity of new technology represented by additional capital stock was almost neutral in this industry group. Results from the same function and the Translog production function show that the growth in total factor productivity from technological improvement throughout the period was, on average, 5.2 per cent. This figure is the fourth highest in the sector. These results may well imply that the technological improvements that contributed to total productivity increases were rooted in factors other than direct increases in capital stock. One such potential factor is changes in economies of scale and other measurements of technological change.

Economies of Scale, Technological Change, Elasticity of Substitution, and Labour Share

Estimation results of the CD and the CES production functions show that this industry group enjoyed economies of scale of 1.4, so that an additional 1 per cent of factor inputs resulted in 1.4 per cent in total output. Our computation of the rate of change in economies of scale shows that the industry experienced an increasing rate of growth from 0.3 per cent per year in the 1960s to 1 per cent per year in the 1970s. The Translog function confirmed these encouraging results (Volume I, Table 3-3), showing similar economies of scale (1.45) as well as growth at an increasing rate through time (see Figure 10-2).

Figure 10-3 plots the technological progress variable (g) of the VES production function, as well as the elasticity of substitution variable. The findings here are entirely consistent with our earlier discussion on technological change in this industry. The technical change variable increased from 0.93 in 1961 to 0.97 in 1977. This means that the technology in this industry is slightly labour saving, but indeed close to neutral. An examination of Table D-6 in Volume I shows that technology did not change at all after 1970, whereas capital intensity increased considerably during that period. Elasticity of substitution fluctuated between 0.86 and 0.89 from 1960 to 1977, indicating that factors of production are not entirely similar in terms of technology and cannot be freely interchanged. Yet if it were equal to 1, factors could be freely substituted leaving production unchanged. The industries are not, however, far from being almost substitutable, and during seventeen years the relative uniqueness of factors of production did not change much.

The share of labour of value added declined from 64 per cent in 1961 to 57 per cent in 1977 (Figure 10-4). Changes in real earnings were greater in periods of increased labour share and smaller in periods of greater capital intensity. In 1976 there was a notable drop in labour share but almost no change in real earnings between 1976 and 1977.

90

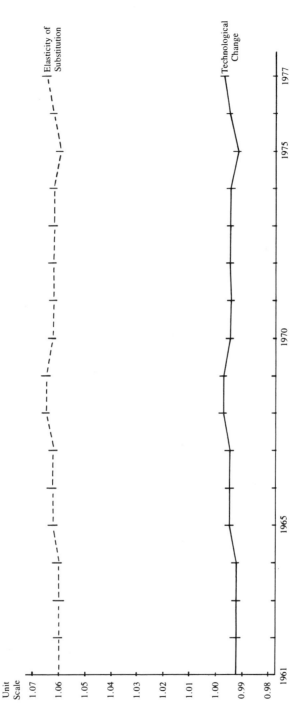

FIGURE 10-3

ELASTICITY OF SUBSTITUTION AND TECHNOLOGICAL CHANGE,

FURNITURE AND FIXTURES INDUSTRIES

(in 1971 constant dollars)

91

92

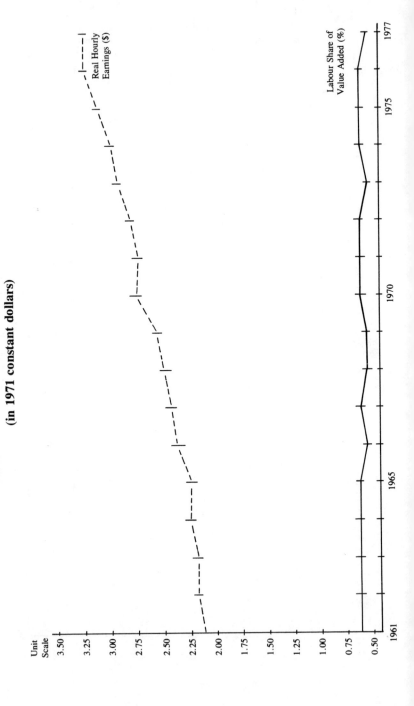

FIGURE 10-4

RATE OF EARNINGS AND LABOUR SHARE OF VALUE ADDED,
FURNITURE AND FIXTURES INDUSTRIES

(in 1971 constant dollars)

While it is difficult to discuss clearly the direction of change in this industry, capital-using technology seems to be on the increase and further capital intensification can likely be expected. It is important, therefore, to investigate why increased capital intensification has not made a significant impact on labour and thus total productivity. Once this question is answered, perhaps new technology that would have a greater impact on productivity could be adopted.

Paper and Paper Products Industries 11

This industry group represents 9.7 per cent of the value added output by the manufacturing sector and employs close to 99,000 workers in 660 establishments. It ranks third in the sector in number of employees per establishment (149), and fourth with respect to value added per establishment.

Capacity Utilization

Figure 11-1 shows this industry group's potential output plotted against actual output, with the gap between these two measuring output forgone because of its inability to utilize its full-capacity production level in each year in the series since 1946. Although the computation, or estimation, of capacity utilization indices involved supply-side variables (capital and output), the resulting indices indirectly reflect fluctuations in market demand both domestically and internationally for the products of an industry. Capacity utilization, therefore, could be quite consistent with fluctuations in the business cycles of the primary markets for the industries' products, mainly Canada and the United States. In order to exhaust the cause and effect relations of capacity utilization patterns, a study of demand for the products should be conducted. However, this is beyond the scope of the research program, which concentrates primarily on the supply side.

Figure 11-1 shows that paper and paper products industries reached full production capacity in 1951, although they had operated relatively close to full capacity until then. In the twenty-six years that followed, they experienced decreasing rates of capacity utilization, getting further and further from their potential output level. The figure shows a V-shaped gap between potential and actual output. The major fluctuations of actual output reflect high and low points of the business cycle — that is, they reflect a slackening market demand — but many

94

FIGURE 11-1
CAPACITY UTILIZATION, PAPER AND PAPER PRODUCTS INDUSTRIES
(in 1971 constant dollars)

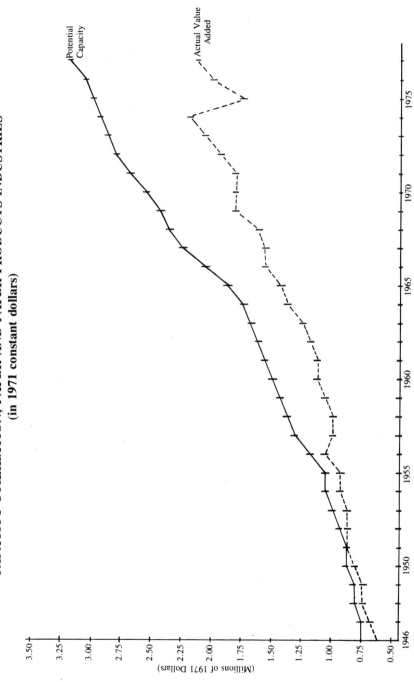

95

other fluctuations also affect production. The low capacity utilization periods occurred in 1958 (72.5 per cent), 1961 (73.7 per cent), 1967 (60.5 per cent), 1970 (70.4 per cent), and 1975 (58.6 per cent). The decline can be attributed not only to a fall in market demand, but also to the rate of capital replacement, the quality of such capital, and productivity.

A more insightful analysis was achieved by thorough observation of the compounded annual rates of change capacity utilization throughout the 1946-77 period. For example, Table 3-2 in Volume I shows that in the 1946-60 period the annual rate of capacity utilization declined by 0.65 per cent per annum. In the 1960s it declined at an annual rate of 0.74 per cent, while in the 1970s the rate was stable at 0.73 per cent annual decline in capacity utilization. In the post-energy crisis years, the industry group experienced an annual rate of decline in its utilization of 1.96 per cent. It placed thirteenth in 1946-60, nineteenth in 1960-70, and tenth in 1970-77 in capacity utilization in the manufacturing sector.

Labour and Capital Productivity, Capital Intensity, and Real Earnings

Table 11-1 shows the average performance of the paper and paper products industry group relative to the sectoral average in terms of the three basic productivity variables. The industries' labour productivity performance fluctuated above the sectoral average from 1946 to 1977 by 2 to 31 per cent. In the 1973-77 subperiod their level of labour productivity was slightly below that of the sector. Their performance relative to all other industries in the sector diminished through time, so that although in the 1947-60 period the paper products industries were fourth in the sector, in the 1960-70 and the 1970-77 periods they retreated to an eighth place and ninth in the sector in the 1973-77 subperiod. The average level of capital intensity in these industries was among the highest in the sector and over twice the total sector average. In the 1950s and in the 1960s this group of industries was the second highest in the sector in terms of capital intensity; in the 1970s, it ranked third in the sector. Real earnings per hour fluctuated between 13 and 18 per cent above the average sectoral level of hourly earnings.

Table 11-2 and Figure 11-2 help to examine the dynamics of the industry group in terms of compounded annual rates of change in the same variables. Rates of growth in total productivity vary for a number of reasons that could be internal or external to the industry (or some combination of both). Internally, they could be the result of changes

96

TABLE 11-1

AVERAGE ANNUAL PERFORMANCE OF LABOUR PRODUCTIVITY,
CAPITAL INTENSITY, AND REAL EARNINGS, PAPER AND PAPER
PRODUCTS INDUSTRIES

	Paper	Total Manu.	Industry/ Sector
	(1971 $/hour)		(%)
Labour Productivity			
1946-77	5.7	4.93	115.6
1946-60	4.6	3.5	131.4
1960-70	6.1	5.3	115.1
1970-77	7.6	7.4	102.7
1970-73	7.7	7.8	98.7
Capital Intensity			
1946-77	13.4	5.6	239.3
1946-60	9.4	4.5	208.9
1960-70	14.8	6.7	220.9
1970-77	19.9	9.1	218.7
1970-73	20.4	9.5	214.7
Real Earnings			
1946-77	3.17	2.8	113.2
1946-60	2.4	2.1	114.3
1960-70	3.4	3.0	113.3
1970-77	4.4	3.8	115.8
1970-73	4.6	3.9	117.9

either in labour or in capital productivity, caused by a significant increase or decrease in labour quality or capital quality and intensity. Changes stemming from external influences could be caused by changes in the relative real prices of inputs; for example, the imposition of high tariffs on imported capital goods or energy price increases.

The annual rate of growth in labour productivity in this industry group remained fairly steady from 1946 to 1970 and rose significantly during the 1970-73 subperiod. From 1973 to 1977 the annual rate of growth in labour productivity fell by 4 percentage points. Throughout the thirty-two-year period the industries' performance was below the sector rate of growth. In terms of annual rates of growth, they ranked

TABLE 11-2

COMPOUNDED ANNUAL RATES OF CHANGE IN LABOUR PRODUCTIVITY, CAPITAL INTENSITY, AND REAL EARNINGS, PAPER AND PAPER PRODUCTS INDUSTRIES

(% in 1971 constant dollars)

	Paper	Total Manu.	Industry/ Sector
Labour Productivity			
1946-77	2.7	3.7	73.0
1946-60	2.8	3.8	73.7
1960-70	2.5	3.6	69.4
1970-77	2.6	3.5	74.3
1970-73	4.8	5.0	96.0
1973-77	0.9	2.4	37.5
Capital Intensity			
1946-77	4.1	3.8	107.9
1946-60	5.3	5.0	106.0
1960-70	3.3	2.3	143.5
1970-77	2.9	3.7	78.4
1970-73	2.2	1.90	105.3
1973-77	3.8	5.01	76.0
Real Earnings			
1946-77	3.4	2.9	117.2
1946-60	3.6	3.3	109.1
1960-70	2.8	2.9	96.6
1970-77	3.9	2.3	169.6
1970-73	3.1	2.7	114.8
1973-77	4.5	2.0	225.0

twelfth in the sector in the 1950s, sixteenth in the 1960s, and seventeenth in the 1970s.

The annual rates of growth in hourly real earnings fluctuated in tune with those in labour productivity only in the main three periods, and when the 1970-77 period was divided into two subperiods, these two variables grew in inverse relation to one another. For example, in the 1970-73 subperiod labour productivity increased by 4.8 per cent per year, 2.2 percentage points higher than in the previous period; however, real earnings increased by only 0.3 percentage points compared with the 1960-70 period. In 1973-77 the growth rate of labour productivity decreased by 3.9 percentage points from the 1970-73 rates of growth, while real earnings increased by 1.4 percentage points. In general, the rates of growth in labour

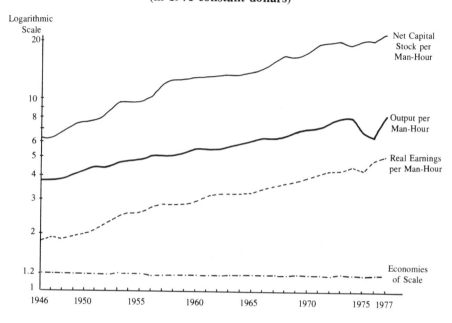

FIGURE 11-2
**RATES OF CHANGE IN LABOUR PRODUCTIVITY, CAPITAL
INTENSITY, REAL EARNINGS, AND ECONOMIES OF SCALE,
PAPER AND PAPER PRODUCTS INDUSTRIES**
(in 1971 constant dollars)

productivity and real earnings should be similar and consistent with one another.

The annual rates of growth in capital intensity do not appear to be consistent with those of productivity growth in any period. In 1960-70 there was a 2.0-percentage-point decline in the rate of growth of capital intensity from the preceding period, while labour productivity rates of growth remained virtually unchanged. In the 1970-77 period annual rates of growth of capital intensity fell a further 0.4 percentage points, while labour productivity remained almost unchanged. From 1970 until 1973 the growth rate of capital intensity declined 1.1 percentage points from that in the 1960-70 period, while the growth rate of labour productivity increased 2.2 percentage points. In the 1973-77 subperiod the situation reversed: the capital intensity growth rate increased by 1.6 percentage points while the growth rate of labour productivity decreased by 3.9 percentage points. In comparison with the sector, these industries' productivity changes were always below those of the

99

sector; real earnings were above the sector; and capital intensity was above the sector until 1970 and then fell.

Figure 11-2 shows the rates of change in these three variables. The relationship between labour productivity and real earnings was not strictly consistent in 1946-54 and in 1972-77; capital intensity changed at rates different from those of labour productivity in the 1950s and from 1966 on.

Table 11-3 exposes some basic issues in productivity analysis. It shows that average productivity to earnings ratios in the industry group were above 1.0 but declined after the 1950s to the sectoral average. At first sight it seems as though labour produced from 80 to 90 per cent more than it took back in real earnings. The averages, however, may be grossly misleading. Therefore, we observe the relationship between productivity and payments to labour as both changed from one year to the next. These industries "overpaid" labour consistently; for example, in the 1946-60 period real earnings per hour increased annually by 30 per cent more than labour productivity per man-hour. In

TABLE 11-3

RATIO OF LABOUR PRODUCTIVITY/EARNINGS, OUTPUT/CAPITAL, AND TECHNOLOGICAL CHANGE,
PAPER AND PAPER PRODUCTS INDUSTRIES

(in 1971 constant dollars)

	1946-77	1946-60	1960-70	1970-77	1970-73	1973-77
	AVERAGE LABOUR PRODUCTIVITY/AVERAGE REAL EARNINGS					
Total manufacturing	1.79	1.69	1.80	1.96		1.99
Paper	1.80	1.93	1.79	1.71		1.68
	COMPOUNDED RATES OF CHANGE IN LABOUR PRODUCTIVITY/REAL EARNINGS					
Total manufacturing	1.30	1.17	1.24	1.53	1.85	1.20
Paper	0.78	0.77	0.90	0.67	1.57	0.21
	AVERAGE OUTPUT/AVERAGE CAPITAL					
Total manufacturing	0.81	0.80	0.81	0.82	0.83	0.82
Paper	0.45	0.50	0.41	0.38	0.39	0.38
	COMPOUNDED RATES OF CHANGE IN OUTPUT/CAPITAL					
Total manufacturing	−0.14	−1.14	1.30	−0.16	2.95	−2.43
Paper	−1.40	−2.39	−0.76	−0.30	1.02	−1.27

	COMPOUNDED RATES OF CHANGE IN TECHNOLOGY (%)		
	1946-77	1960-70	1970-77
Total manufacturing	0.271	0.259	0.361
Paper	0.127	0.099	0.278

the 1960s the situation improved, when labour's real earnings increased only 11 per cent more than its productivity. In the 1970s the rate of change in real earnings was greater by half than the annual rate of change in productivity. This situation was decidedly harmful to the industries' competitive and profit position. Labour received unjustifiably high earnings rate increases that were not the fruits of its contribution to direct productivity. This phenomenon is generally the main cause for upward pressure on prices, since excess purchasing power is provided to labour.

The average output-capital ratios in this industry group were very low relative to the sector levels (about 50 per cent). The most serious shortcoming of this group, however, was the *negative* rates of growth in capital productivity. In the 1950s it ranked fifteenth in the sector in terms of capital productivity and in the 1960s it ranked eighteenth. But in the 1970s capital productivity in the group improved considerably, moving up to tenth place. No doubt the declining productivity of capital was an important source of lagging labour and total productivity in this industry.

The ineffectiveness of capital as a contributory factor to labour productivity is confirmed by estimates of m, which measures the impact of technology on labour efficiency in the VES production function. This variable is in fact the elasticity of the response of labour to the introduction of new technology in new capital. Table 3-11 in Volume I shows this m coefficient to be 0.21, which is next to the lowest in the manufacturing sector and means that an increase of 1 per cent in technology had an impact of 0.2 per cent on labour efficiency. A plausible explanation for such an insignificant effect is that the type of "new" technology that was introduced in, say, 1965 was not significantly different from "old" production technology. Thus the quality of capital did not vary significantly over time in the paper products industries, which began to show diminishing productivity rates.

Technological Change, Elasticity of Substitution, Labour Share, and Economies of Scale

In the paper industries the annual rate of change in technology was positive and increasing, progressing towards capital-saving technology (Table 11-3). Figure 11-3 shows a more detailed picture of the industries' technological progress from 1946 to 1977. The industries' technology was "neutral" until 1953, when they began to experience a slight tendency towards labour-using technology with some small

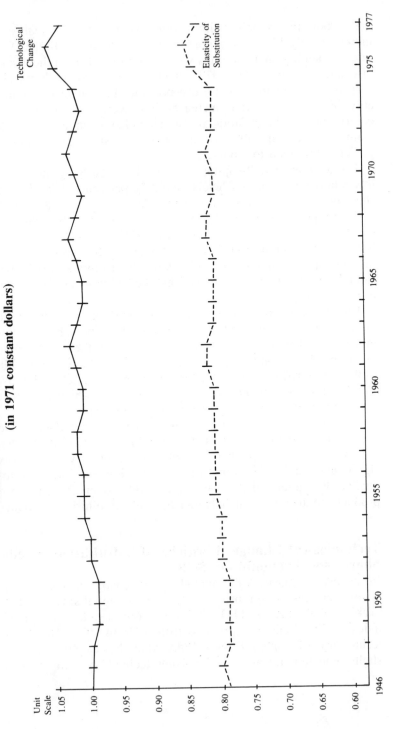

FIGURE 11-3
ELASTICITY OF SUBSTITUTION AND TECHNOLOGICAL CHANGE,
PAPER AND PAPER PRODUCTS INDUSTRIES
(in 1971 constant dollars)

fluctuations. The greatest value, 1.06, was reached in 1976. In 1977 the value of the technical progress variable dropped 2 per cent, indicating a slight change of direction towards capital-using technology. In the statistical estimations of the four production functions, the average contribution of technology to total productivity for the thirty-two-year period was a statistically insignificant 1.7 per cent (see the Translog production function in Volume I, Table D-4).

The ease with which factors of production (capital and labour) can be substituted by one another without reducing the level of total production was estimated by the VES production function. The variable elasticity of substitution, plotted in Figure 11-3, is quite consistent with the technical progress variable: from 1946 to 1960, it fluctuated between 0.79 and 0.81 and from 1960 to 1974 the fluctuations were between 0.81 and 0.82. From 1974 to 1976 the variable changed from 0.81 to 0.85, and in 1977 it dropped back to 0.83. When the value of the variable elasticity of substitution is significantly less than one, the factors of production are dissimilar and hence are not easily substituted without jeopardising the overall level of production. It is rather surprising to discover that changes in capital intensity in these industries, mainly in 1970-73, did not reduce the values of the elasticity of substitution or the technological progress function. Perhaps the explanation lies in the fact that the time lag needed to see the effects of capital intensification in these industries is at least four to five years.

Figure 11-4 shows the rates of change in real earnings and labour share of value added. Since capital and labour are the two factors in our production function, their shares in output total 100 per cent. The figure shows that labour share increased from 49 per cent in 1946 to 54 per cent in 1960. In the 1960s it increased from 54 per cent to 56 per cent, and in the 1970-76 period it continued to increase from 54 per cent to 65 per cent. From 1976 to 1977 there was a 4 per cent decline in labour share. On the whole, the share of labour increased steadily throughout the thirty-two-year period, and thus the share of capital declined. Real earnings increased throughout the period as well, with only one decline in 1975.

The relationship between productivity and economies of scale is important. The paper and paper products industries enjoyed economies of scale of 1.2 throughout the whole period, although estimates of this variable from the CES production function showed they rose insignificantly from 1.219 in 1946 to 1.220 in 1977. The Translog production function recorded identical behaviour. Diwan's test shows

103

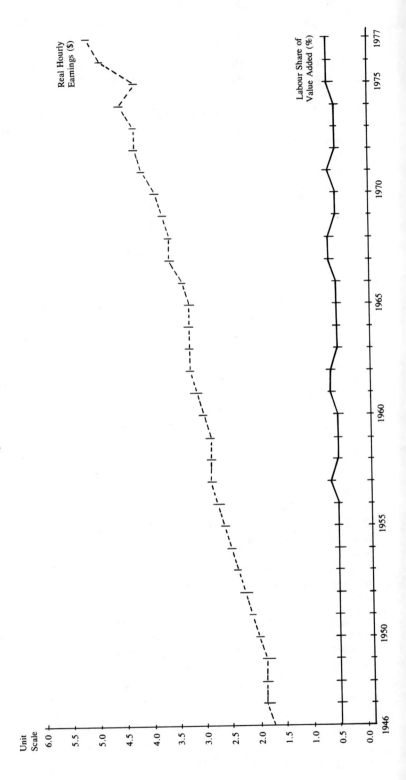

FIGURE 11-4
RATE OF EARNINGS AND LABOUR SHARE OF VALUE ADDED,
PAPER AND PAPER PRODUCTS INDUSTRIES
(in 1971 constant dollars)

Real Hourly
Earnings ($)

Labour Share of
Value Added (%)

Unit
Scale

6.0
5.5
5.0
4.5
4.0
3.5
3.0
2.5
2.0
1.5
1.0
0.5
0.0

1946   1950   1955   1960   1965   1970   1975   1977

that economies of scale have contributed only 1.3 per cent to labour productivity. Thus in this industry economies of scale bear no relationship to productivity performance and short product runs are a possible constraint on achieving optimal, least-cost production. The answer to such a problem is, of course, to rationalize production by reducing diversification in production lines. Although there is no way to gauge the proper scale for this or any other industry, except through an exhaustive industry study, the objective is to attain a minimum unit cost in producing a given product. For some industries the optimal level of production could well be in small-scale operations.

Printing, Publishing and Allied Industries   **12**

The printing and publishing industry group represents 5.4 of the sector value added and employs 55,000 employees in 3,427 establishments. It ranks the lowest in the sector in the number of employees per establishment, and eighteenth in value added per establishment.

Capacity Utilization

Figure 12-1 shows the industry potential output plotted against actual output. In general, this figure indicates that this industry group operated most of the period rather close to its full capacity, although fluctuations of varying magnitudes occurred in different periods along the three-decade time span. Specifically, capacity utilization converged from 65 per cent in 1946 to 100 per cent in 1956. From 1956 to 1964 the capacity utilization rate diminished somewhat to 90.6 per cent. In the 1964-74 decade a clear increase in capacity utilization emerged and the industry reached a 99 per cent utilization in 1973 and 98 per cent in 1974. The rate of utilization declined for the next three years to 95 per cent in 1977. A computation of the compounded annual rates of change in capacity utilization places the industry group above the sectoral performance in the 1950s and the 1970s but below it in the 1960s (see Volume I, Table 3-2).

Labour Productivity, Capital Intensity, and Real Earnings

Table 12-1 shows the industry's annual average labour productivity, capital intensity, and real earnings compared with average performance in total manufacturing. Labour productivity in this industry group outperformed that in the sector in the 1950s and the 1960s, but equalled it in the 1970s. The group ranked eighth in average performance in the 1950s, ninth in the 1960s, and tenth in the 1970s; in the post-1973 era it slipped to a twelfth place. The average level of capital intensity was below the sector average throughout, declining

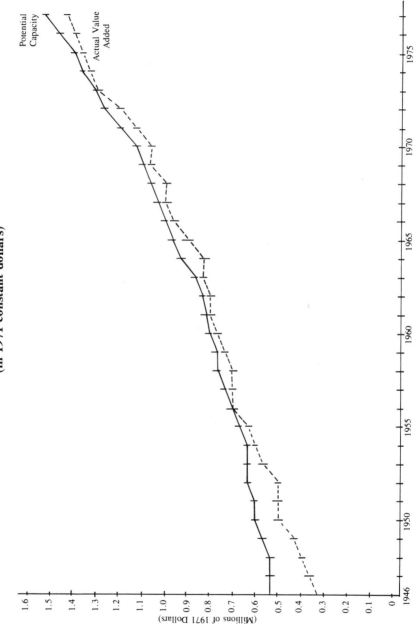

FIGURE 12-1

CAPACITY UTILIZATION, PRINTING, PUBLISHING AND ALLIED INDUSTRIES

(in 1971 constant dollars)

Potential Capacity

Actual Value Added

(Millions of 1971 Dollars)

107

TABLE 12-1

**AVERAGE ANNUAL PERFORMANCE OF LABOUR PRODUCTIVITY,
CAPITAL INTENSITY, AND REAL EARNINGS,
PRINTING, PUBLISHING AND ALLIED INDUSTRIES**

	Printing and Publishing	Total Manu.	Industry/ Sector
	(1971 $/hour)		(%)
Labour Productivity			
1946-77	5.36	4.93	108.7
1946-60	4.10	3.50	117.1
1960-70	5.72	5.34	107.1
1970-77	7.53	7.43	101.3
1973-77	7.91	7.79	101.5
Capital Intensity			
1946-77	3.90	5.58	69.9
1946-60	2.93	4.47	65.5
1960-70	4.29	6.67	64.3
1970-77	5.41	9.11	59.4
1973-77	5.58	9.53	58.3
Real Earnings			
1946-77	3.04	2.75	110.5
1946-60	2.24	2.07	108.2
1960-70	3.33	2.96	112.5
1970-77	4.24	3.79	111.9
1973-77	4.41	3.92	112.5

from 66 per cent of the sectoral level in the 1950s to 59 per cent in the 1970s.

The relative levels of real earnings per hour paid ranked higher within the sector than the corresponding labour productivity levels; that is, in the 1950s the industry group ranked sixth in the sector, and in the 1960s and the 1970s it maintained a seventh place in earnings levels. A comparison with the average sector earnings level shows the industry level to be 8 per cent higher than that in the sector in the 1950s and 12 per cent above the sectoral average in the following two decades.

But average levels of these variables should be handled very cautiously, because they do not show the dynamics of the industry through time and thus are not very useful for policy formation. However, they do show relationships among variables and provide some hints as to what should be focused on in a rate of change analysis.

For example, we learn that levels of capital intensity and labour productivity were not strictly consistent with one another, but that they moved generally in the same direction. The group's rank in the sector is higher for labour productivity than capital intensity. Its relative position in terms of real earnings was higher than in terms of average labour productivity.

Tracing the annual rates of growth of these relationships gave more complete and useful data for policy analysis. Table 12-2 shows that the annual rate of growth in labour productivity decreased from 3.47 per cent in the 1950s to 2.58 per cent in the 1960s. In the 1970s it increased 3.67 per cent, and was for the first time above the sector's

TABLE 12-2

COMPOUNDED ANNUAL RATES OF CHANGE IN LABOUR PRODUCTIVITY, CAPITAL INTENSITY, AND REAL EARNINGS, PRINTING, PUBLISHING AND ALLIED INDUSTRIES

(% in 1971 constant dollars)

	Printing and Publishing	Total Manu.	Industry/ Sector
Labour Productivity			
1946-77	3.23	3.70	87.3
1946-60	3.47	3.82	90.8
1960-70	2.58	3.64	70.9
1970-77	3.67	3.53	104.0
1970-73	3.55	5.04	70.4
1973-77	3.76	2.41	156.0
Capital Intensity			
1946-77	2.81	3.83	73.4
1946-60	2.74	4.99	54.9
1960-70	2.95	2.34	126.1
1970-77	2.76	3.66	75.4
1970-73	0.99	1.90	52.1
1973-77	4.11	5.01	82.0
Real Earnings			
1946-77	3.10	2.85	108.8
1946-60	3.44	3.27	105.2
1960-70	2.88	2.94	98.0
1970-77	2.71	2.31	117.3
1970-73	2.29	2.72	84.2
1973-77	3.02	2.01	150.2

rate of growth. Dividing the period 1970-77 into two subperiods revealed that the industry experienced a higher rate of annual growth in labour productivity in the 1973-77 subperiod than in the 1970-73 subperiod. In the post-energy crisis years the industry's rates of annual growth were 1.5 times those of the sector's. The results of this table show that a slight slowdown in the rise in labour productivity occurred in the pre-energy crisis subperiod. But unlike the slowdown in growth for total manufacturing, there was a rise in the growth rate of labour productivity in this industry in 1973-77. The productivity growth of the industry placed it twelfth in the 1950s and sixteenth in the following two decades.

Looking at the relationship between capital intensity and labour productivity in each industry classification so far has provided no significant evidence that a decline in capital intensity was the major cause of the production slowdown. The paper and paper products industry group provides no further support for that proposition. Table 12-2 shows that the annual rate of growth in capital intensity increased by 0.21 percentage points from the 1950s to the 1960s, while for the same two periods the annual rate of growth in labour productivity decreased by 0.9 percentage points annually. The annual rate of growth from the 1960s to the 1970s shows the same inconsistency. Labour productivity increased by 1.1 percentage points, while growth in capital intensity decreased by 0.2 percentage points.

By contrast the fluctuations in annual rates of growth in real earnings per hour and changes in productivity growth were consistent with one another in the 1950s and in the 1960s. However, a comparison of the rates of growth in the 1960s and the 1970s presents some difficulties. There was an annual decrease in the rate of growth in real earnings in the 1970s, while the growth in labour productivity showed an increase for the same period. The difficulty arises in observing the "inconsistency" because economists expect labour productivity and real earnings always to change in the same proportions; that is, on the margin, labour should receive its marginal product in real terms. Figure 12-2 provides a convenient display of the relationship among these three variables and shows that the relationship between labour productivity and real earnings was not strictly consistent. It also shows that fluctuations in the rate of growth in capital intensity did not coincide with, or were not followed by, similar fluctuations in labour productivity.

Table 12-3 provides the numbers denoting the relationships between labour productivity and real earnings for each period; it also gives

110

FIGURE 12-2
RATES OF CHANGE IN LABOUR PRODUCTIVITY, CAPITAL
INTENSITY, REAL EARNINGS, AND ECONOMIES OF SCALE,
PRINTING, PUBLISHING AND ALLIED PRODUCTS INDUSTRIES
(in 1971 constant dollars)

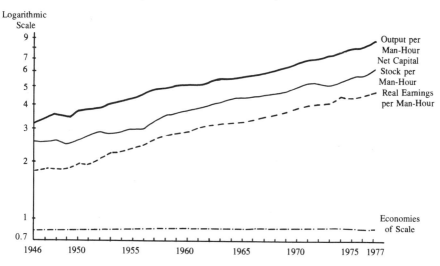

explicit numerical results of the productivity of capital, a factor overlooked by most studies on productivity. The table reveals that the ratios of average labour productivity to real earnings levels were well above one throughout all the periods. Thus the average labour contribution to productivity exceeded payments to labour by the industry. This ratio was above the sectoral ratio in the 1950s and below it in the following two decades, with labour producing 72 to 83 per cent more than it took back in earnings. Again, however, average levels do not reflect what is sought after in labour negotiations and government policy formation, for regardless of the starting levels, the real question is whether changes in productivity were consistent with changes in the rate of growth of real earnings. Table 12-3 shows that in the 1950s the rate of growth in labour productivity was equivalent to the growth rate in real earnings. In the 1960s, however, the annual rate of growth in real earnings was 11 per cent greater than that in labour productivity — or labour received 11 per cent more in real earnings than it produced. In the 1970-77 period this situation reversed: the rate of growth in real earnings was only 74 per cent of the rate of growth in productivity and labour received in real earnings only 74 per cent of its

111

TABLE 12-3

RATIO OF LABOUR PRODUCTIVITY/EARNINGS, OUTPUT/CAPITAL, AND TECHNOLOGICAL CHANGE, PRINTING, PUBLISHING AND ALLIED INDUSTRIES

(in 1971 constant dollars)

	1946-77	1946-60	1960-70	1970-77	1970-73	1973-77
	AVERAGE LABOUR PRODUCTIVITY/AVERAGE REAL EARNINGS					
Total manufacturing	1.79	1.69	1.80	1.96		1.99
Printing and Publishing	1.76	1.83	1.72	1.78		1.79
	COMPOUNDED RATES OF CHANGE IN LABOUR PRODUCTIVITY/REAL EARNINGS					
Total manufacturing	1.30	1.17	1.24	1.53	1.85	1.20
Printing and Publishing	1.04	1.01	0.90	1.35	1.55	1.25
	AVERAGE OUTPUT/AVERAGE CAPITAL					
Total manufacturing	0.81	0.80	0.81	0.82	0.83	0.82
Printing and Publishing	1.38	1.39	1.33	1.39	1.37	1.42
	COMPOUNDED RATES OF CHANGE IN OUTPUT/CAPITAL					
Total manufacturing	−0.14	−1.14	1.30	−0.16	2.95	−2.43
Printing and Publishing	0.41	0.72	−0.33	0.87	2.50	−0.33

	COMPOUNDED RATES OF CHANGE IN TECHNOLOGY (%)		
	1946-77	1960-70	1970-77
Total manufacturing	0.271	0.259	0.361
Printing and Publishing	0	0	0

direct contribution to productivity. Clearly, labour has not contributed to any pressure on prices because of demands for wage increases.

The average levels of capital productivity in this industry group were stable and significantly above the sector average throughout all periods, placing it in about the middle of the sector. The annual rates of change give a different picture. In the 1950s, the rate of growth in average capital productivity was positive and increasing by 0.7 per cent per annum, whereas in the manufacturing sector as a whole, the average productivity of capital declined at a rate of 1.1 per cent per year. In the 1960s the inverse was the case. Average productivity in the industry declined at a rate of 0.3 per cent per annum, while that of the sector increased by 1.3 per cent per year. In the 1970s the rate of growth in capital productivity increased in the industry by 0.9 per cent per annum, while that of the sector decreased by 0.2 per cent. The industry group's ranking within the sector is lower in terms of the rates of growth than in terms of levels: in the 1950s they ranked twelfth; in the 1960s, thirteenth; and in the 1970s, eleventh.

Changes in the stock of capital generally indicate changes in the technology of production, because newly added capital embodies new technology and is presumed to exert some impact on labour efficiency and productivity. The VES production function measures the impact of technology on labour efficiency, where m is the elasticity of the response of labour efficiency to the introduction of new technology. Table 3-11 in Volume I shows the value of m to be 0.85 for this industry group, which ranks it eleventh in the sector. This means that a 1 per cent increase in new technology had an impact of 0.85 per cent on labour efficiency in the period.

Technological Change, Elasticity of Substitution, Labour Share, and Economies of Scale

The technological progress variable, g, provides information on the type of technology used by the industry in its production process. A value less than one implies capital-using technology; greater than one implies a labour-using technology. Table 12-3 shows that the annual rate of change in technology of production was zero throughout all periods. The more detailed account of the industry's technological progress from 1946 to 1977 in Figure 12-3 shows that the industry's technology was "neutral" throughout. Our statistical estimations of the VES and the CES production functions verify these results by showing that capital was statistically insignificant in its contributions to total factor productivity, and that the contribution of technology to total factor productivity growth was 0.3 per cent, compared with the 2.9 per cent of the sectoral average (see Volume I, Appendix D).

The ease with which factors of production can be substituted by one another without reducing the level of total productivity was estimated using the VES production function. This variable elasticity of substitution of the biased type is plotted in Figure 12-3 and is consistent with the type of technology used by the printing and publishing industries; that is, the low value — around 0.94 throughout the period — means that factors of production were quite similar and by and large substitutable.

Figure 12-4 shows the rate of change in real earnings and that of labour share of value added. Since labour and capital are the two factors of production involved, the shares of labour and capital add up to 100 per cent. This figure demonstrates that labour share fluctuated up to 1958 when it was 56 per cent. From 1958 to 1976 the share of labour was almost constant with variations of 2 to 3 per cent. In 1977 it

113

FIGURE 12-3
ELASTICITY OF SUBSTITUTION AND TECHNOLOGICAL CHANGE,
PRINTING, PUBLISHING AND ALLIED INDUSTRIES
(in 1971 constant dollars)

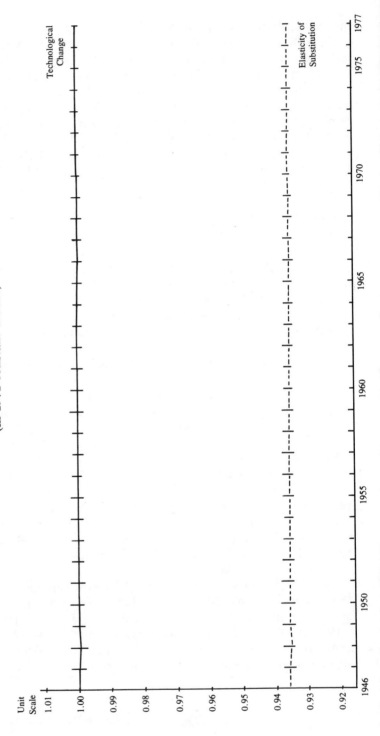

FIGURE 12-4

RATE OF EARNINGS AND LABOUR SHARE OF VALUE ADDED, PRINTING, PUBLISHING AND ALLIED INDUSTRIES

(in 1971 constant dollars)

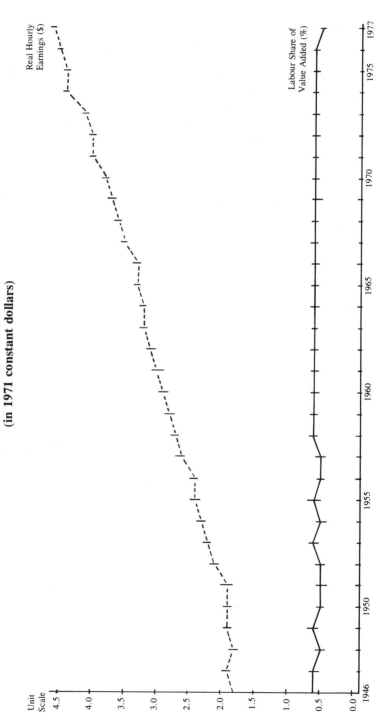

decreased to 54 per cent, which matches the 1957 level in this industry.

On average this industry group enjoyed economies of scale of 1.6 throughout the whole period. It is possible, however, that because of the aggregation of this group, specific scale problems of a subgroup, such as publishing, are hidden. The Diwan test shows that economies of scale contributed an average of 23 per cent (Volume I, Table 3-10) to the growth in labour productivity. Statistical tests of the Translog production function show that economies of scale rose but in a statistically insignificant way. The computations of annual levels of economies of scale from the CES production function (Volume I, Table 3-4) show slight growth in this variable through time, of which most occurred in recent years. On the evidence of these tests, there is no connection between changes in economies of scale and productivity growth.

Primary Metals Industries

13

The primary metals industry group represents 7.7 per cent of total manufacturing value added and employs about 89,000 employees in 382 establishments. The average number of employees per establishment is 230, and the industry group ranks third in the sector in terms of value added per establishment.

Capacity Utilization

Figure 13-1 shows the industry's actual and potential capacity output. The difference between these two indicates the utilized capacity through time, and thus output or income forgone. This figure reveals that the primary metals industry group reached its full capacity output in 1965, from a low of 81.7 per cent in 1961. From 1965 on, capacity utilization fluctuated considerably, falling to 85 per cent in 1972, rising to a high of 91 per cent in 1974, declining again to its lowest point of 74 per cent in 1976, and recovering to a 77 per cent utilization in 1977. A comparison of the industry with total manufacturing shows that in the 1960-70 period the sector increased its capacity utilization by an annual rate of 1.15 per cent, while the primary metals industry increased its capacity utilization by 1.38 per cent per year. In the 1970-77 period, capacity utilization decreased in the sector by 0.34 per cent per annum, while the primary metals industry decreased its rate by 2.50 per cent per year. After the energy crisis, however, the sector's capacity utilization rate recorded an annual decrease of 2.57 per cent, whereas the industry's annual rate of decrease was 3.29 per cent. Once again this excess capacity indicates a less than optimal allocation of productive resources that impedes the efficient use of capital and labour. Clearly, this industry experienced an above average setback in its ability to utilize its potential capacity after 1973. It is, therefore, interesting to observe whether this setback was transferred to a slowdown in productivity and capital intensity.

117

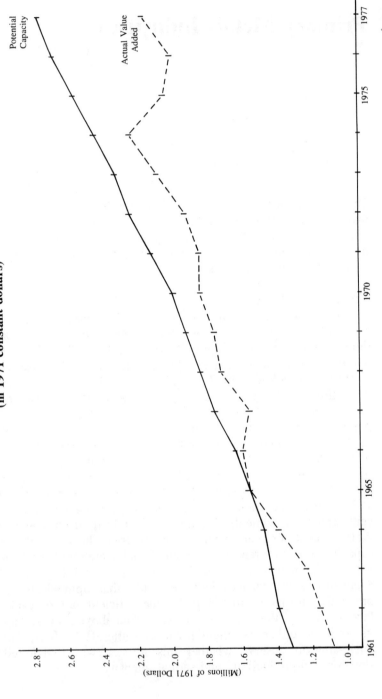

FIGURE 13-1

CAPACITY UTILIZATION, PRIMARY METALS INDUSTRIES

(in 1971 constant dollars)

118

Labour Productivity, Capital Intensity, and Real Earnings

Table 13-1 compares the industry's average performance in labour productivity, capital intensity, and real earnings. The average performance of labour productivity in the primary metals industries group was above the sectoral average by 26 per cent in the 1960s and by 10 per cent in the 1970s. Average levels of capital intensity in the group were consistently almost double the sectoral average after 1960. Comparing the change in average levels in both variables shows a 22 per cent increase in average labour productivity from the 1960s to the 1970s, and a 26 per cent increase in the level of capital intensity in the same period. The relative position of this group in the sector was fifth in average labour productivity in the 1960s and sixth in the 1970s; it was third in average capital intensity in the 1960s and fourth in the 1970s. Average levels of real earnings in the industry in the 1960-70 period were 21.6 per cent higher than in the sector, and 19 per cent higher than the sectoral average in the 1970s. There seems to be a consistency in the trends and magnitudes of change in the average

TABLE 13-1

AVERAGE ANNUAL PERFORMANCE OF LABOUR PRODUCTIVITY, CAPITAL INTENSITY, AND REAL EARNINGS, PRIMARY METALS INDUSTRIES

	Primary Metals	Total Manu.	Industry/ Sector
	(1971 $/hour)		(%)
Labour Productivity			
1960-77	7.44	6.39	
1960-70	6.70	5.34	125.5
1970-77	8.18	7.43	110.1
1973-77	8.44	7.79	108.3
Capital Intensity			
1960-77	16.09	7.89	
1960-70	14.24	6.67	213.5
1970-77	17.94	9.11	196.9
1973-77	18.83	9.53	197.6
Real Earnings			
1960-77	4.06	3.38	
1960-70	3.60	2.96	121.6
1970-77	4.52	3.79	119.3
1973-77	4.70	3.92	119.9

levels of these three variables, a phenomenon absent in most other industries so far.

For further insight into the rates of growth of these three variables, we turn to Table 13-2 and Figure 13-2. The table shows that the annual rate of growth in labour productivity was consistently below that of the sector in the four periods: in the 1960s, it was 83 per cent of the sector's annual rate of growth; in the 1970s it declined to 55 per cent. When the 1970-77 period was divided into two subperiods it appeared that there was a significant decline in the rate of growth of labour productivity in the 1973-77 period. This is consistent with the decline in capacity utilization during the same period.

The annual rates of growth in capital intensity were not all consistent with those of labour productivity. The relationship between these variables is best viewed in Figure 13-2. In the 1970s the industry

TABLE 13-2

COMPOUNDED ANNUAL RATES OF CHANGE IN LABOUR PRODUCTIVITY, CAPITAL INTENSITY, AND REAL EARNINGS, PRIMARY METALS INDUSTRIES

(% in 1971 constant dollars)

	Primary Metals	Total Manu.	Industry/ Sector
Labour Productivity			
1960-77	2.48	3.59	
1960-70	3.01	3.64	82.7
1970-77	1.95	3.53	55.2
1970-73	3.78	5.04	75.0
1973-77	0.59	2.41	24.5
Capital Intensity			
1960-77	2.54	3.00	
1960-70	1.22	2.34	52.1
1970-77	3.85	3.66	105.2
1970-73	3.69	1.90	73.7
1973-77	4.05	5.01	80.4
Real Earnings			
1960-77	2.41	2.63	
1960-70	1.96	2.94	66.7
1970-77	2.85	2.31	123.4
1970-73	3.93	2.72	144.5
1973-77	2.05	2.01	102.0

120

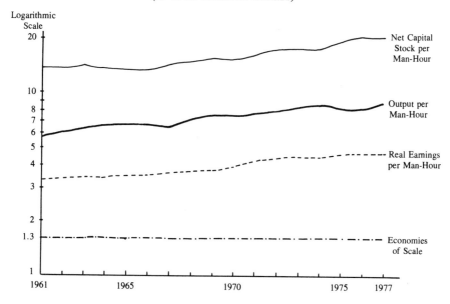

FIGURE 13-2
**RATES OF CHANGE IN LABOUR PRODUCTIVITY, CAPITAL
INTENSITY, REAL EARNINGS, AND ECONOMIES OF SCALE,
PRIMARY METALS INDUSTRIES**
(in 1971 constant dollars)

experienced an increase of 2.63 percentage points in the annual rate of growth of capital intensity over the 1960s, while the annual rate of growth in labour productivity declined by 1.06 percentage points for the same periods. When the 1970-77 period is divided into two subperiods, 1970-73 and 1973-77, we see that there was an increase in the annual rate of growth of capital intensity from the first to the second subperiod, while for the same subperiods labour productivity declined 3.19 percentage points annually.

The patterns of change in labour productivity and real earnings were also not consistent with one another. As the rate of growth in labour productivity declined in the 1970s from that in the 1960s, the rate of growth in real earnings increased from 66 per cent of the sectoral rate in the 1960s to 123 per cent of it in the 1970s. These important relationships are captured in Table 13-3. The annual average ratios of productivity to real earnings were 1.86 in the 1960s and 1.81 in the 1970s. This means that, on average, during these decades the levels of labour earnings were 54 per cent and 55 per cent of that of labour

TABLE 13-3

RATIO OF LABOUR PRODUCTIVITY/EARNINGS, OUTPUT/CAPITAL, AND TECHNOLOGICAL CHANGE, PRIMARY METALS INDUSTRIES

(in 1971 constant dollars)

	1960-77	1960-70	1970-77	1970-73	1973-77
AVERAGE LABOUR PRODUCTIVITY/AVERAGE REAL EARNINGS					
Total manufacturing	1.92	1.80	1.96		1.99
Primary Metals	1.82	1.86	1.81		1.80
COMPOUNDED RATES OF CHANGE IN LABOUR PRODUCTIVITY/REAL EARNINGS					
Total manufacturing	1.39	1.24	1.53	1.85	1.20
Primary Metals	1.11	1.54	0.68	0.96	0.29
AVERAGE OUTPUT/AVERAGE CAPITAL					
Total manufacturing	0.82	0.81	0.82	0.83	0.82
Primary Metals	0.67	0.88	0.46	0.47	0.45
COMPOUNDED RATES OF CHANGE IN OUTPUT/CAPITAL					
Total manufacturing	0.57	1.30	−0.16	2.95	−2.43
Primary Metals	−0.02	1.78	−1.82	−0.27	−2.96
COMPOUNDED RATES OF CHANGE IN TECHNOLOGY (%)					
	1960-77	1960-70	1970-77		
Total manufacturing	0.310	0.259	0.361		
Primary Metals	0.212	0.982	−0.769		

productivity, respectively. In the 1960s the industry's average level of this ratio was slightly above the sector's.

Averages are interesting when one's interest lies in performance levels only, but a complete account of productivity behaviour calls for rates of growth throughout the period. The compounded annual rate of growth of the same productivity to earnings ratio reflects changes in the industry's productivity relative to changes in its payments to labour (all in real terms), and also embodies external influences on the industry by product and labour markets. In the 1960s the ratio of the rate of change in productivity to that of to marginal earnings per hour assumed an annual rate of change of 1.54 per cent, compared with 1.24 in the sector. This means that the rate of growth in real earnings lagged 54 per cent behind that of productivity during that decade. In the 1970s, however, that situation reversed and the rate of growth in real earnings was 1.47 faster than that of labour productivity; that is, labour in this industry received annual increases in real earnings that were

1.47 times its contribution to the rate of growth in productivity. Thus this industry group "overpaid" labour beyond the income accrued from a rise in productivity. In the post-1973 period, labour was overpaid by a factor of 3.5.

To an economist, labour received 3.5 times the rate of increase in its productivity, and gains in productivity were lost through uncalled-for increases in real earnings. If the demand for this industry's products were price elastic, there is a high probability that such industry would sustain great losses and perhaps cease to operate. But this industry has a classic oligopolistic structure, and the demand for its products is highly inelastic. Therefore, these inevitable price increases, which compensate for rapidly rising labour earnings, are mostly transferred to consumers who are forced to accept them. It is clear that such a process significantly contributes to inflationary pressures, particularly when the industry directly affects the price structure of hundreds of other industries involved in the production of appliances and cars and in construction.

Since pure competition and, with it, free trade are virtually nonexistent in today's society, government intervention is necessary to help this industry group "normalize" its operation or rationalize its productivity-wage relation for the sake of price stability. I consider this a top priority for governments, because this is a structural approach to combat inflation that will bear far more lasting effects on price stability than the present dangerous practice of manipulating monetary variables through daily accounting exercises.

Since this industry group had almost the highest capital intensity in the sector, and new capital stock (plant and equipment) is a proxy for new production technology, it is important to examine the productivity of capital and the impact of technology on labour efficiency in this industry. Table 13-3 provides some insight, showing that in the 1960s the annual rate of growth in the output-capital ratio was positive and larger than that of the sector. This means that the rate of change in capital productivity was positive and increasing, although ranking approximately mid-sector. In the 1970-77 period, however, this industry group experienced negative growth in capital productivity to the tune of 1.82 per cent per year. The most severe situation occurred after the energy crisis when the annual rate of growth of capital productivity was -2.96 per cent, despite the high annual rate of growth in capital intensity (4.05 per cent). This phenomenon is quite puzzling and thus hard to explain. Nevertheless, it seems that negative capital productivity was a major source of declining labour productivity in this industry, which, of course, prompts us to look at some indicators of the quality of capital in this industry.

Evidence from our estimates of the VES production function shows that total factor productivity growth attributable to technological improvement over time in this industry group during the 1961-77 period was 2.57 per cent compared with the sectoral average of 2.9 per cent. (See Volume I, Tables 3-16 and D-3.) The interesting strategic question is how these industries would respond to new technology embodied in their changing stock of capital. An answer to this policy-oriented question stems from our results obtained from the m parameter of the VES production function. The tests, of course, represent the historical behaviour of the industry, and any attempts to predict the industry's response to new technology should be accompanied with proper qualifications. Nevertheless the value of m for the primary metals industry group is 1.32 (see Volume I, Table 3-11), the fifth largest in the manufacturing sector. This means that an addition of 1 per cent in new technology in this industry group had—and perhaps would have—an impact of 1.32 per cent on increased labour efficiency. Conversely, a deterioration of technology as capital stock depleted would have a more than proportional (1:1.32) negative impact on labour efficiency.

Technological Change, Elasticity of Substitution, Labour Share, and Economies of Scale

The technological progress variable, g, signifies the type and direction of technology utilized by the industry (or firm) in its production process. Table 13-3 shows that the primary metals industry's technical rate of change during the 1960s tended to be labour using, whereas during the 1970s it tended to be capital using. Figure 13-3 displays a finer detailed picture of the industry's technical progress since 1961. The industry's technology was all along of the capital-using type (or labour-saving type), for it fluctuated between 0.85 and 0.97. The figure also shows that fluctuations were not trivial within the boundaries of such technology: three major troughs indicating capital-using technology extremes are shown in 1967, 1972, and 1976; and two main peaks indicating relatively capital-saving technology are shown in 1969 and 1974. When g is computed for the 1970-76 period, it shows an annual rate of growth of capital-using technology of 1.84 per cent, while with the inclusion of 1977 it shows only 0.77 per cent per year. As the figure indicates, 1977 started a new direction towards labour-using technology.

124

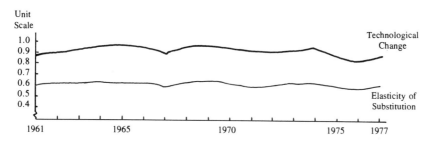

FIGURE 13-3
ELASTICITY OF SUBSTITUTION AND TECHNOLOGICAL
CHANGE, PRIMARY METALS INDUSTRIES
(in 1971 constant dollars)

The ease with which factors of production can be substituted by one another (within a given technology) without reducing total production, is estimated by the elasticity of substitution variable. The results used for this analysis come from the VES production function, because it allows the elasticity of substitution to vary over time and to assume any values the data requires. With a capital-intensive technology factors are not easily substitutable without reducing total output. Over seventeen years, the values of this variable in this industry fluctuated between 0.59 in 1976 and 0.64 in the 1964-66 and 1973-74 periods, indicating clearly a technology in which factors of production cannot be easily replaced without reducing total output. The peaks and troughs are consistent with those of the technological progress function.

Figure 13-4 shows the pattern of change in real earnings and that of the labour share of real earnings in value added. In the figure the labour share was relatively stable from 1961 to 1967 (58 per cent and 56 per cent respectively); it follows that during that period the capital share was between 42 and 44 per cent of value added. In 1968 the labour share dropped to 52 per cent and, while fluctuating slightly upward, converged back to 52 per cent in 1973. The 1973-77 subperiod showed a 5 per cent increase in labour share. Real earnings increased much faster in the 1970s than in the 1960s. In the 1961-70 period the compounded annual rate of growth in real earnings was 2.0 per cent, whereas in 1969-70 that annual rate of growth accelerated to 2.9 per cent. This pattern is not consistent with the rate of growth in labour productivity; that is, the rate of growth in real earnings in the 1960s was 1.05 per cent *below* the rate of productivity growth, while in the

125

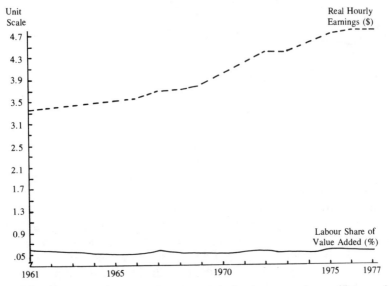

1970s it was 0.9 per cent per annum *above* the annual rate of growth in labour productivity.

As in some of the other industries the primary metals group experienced economies of scale during the 1961-77 period at an average of 1.38. As Figure 13-2 and Table 3-4 in Volume I show, the level of economies of scale in this industry did not change significantly during the period. The Translog production function, designed to test the behaviour of economies of scale through time in a more rigorous way than the CES function, shows that economies of scale grew at a declining rate during the period and in a statistically significant way (see Volume I, Table 3-6). If such trend continues, as time progresses an increase in inputs would yield a smaller return in output. Applying the Diwan test (see Volume I, Table 3-10) to identify the contribution of economies of scale to growth in labour productivity, I found that contribution to be 24 per cent, compared with 31 per cent for the sector. Within the sector the industry ranks fourth in terms of contribution of economies of scale to productivity growth. There is, therefore, no clearcut relationship in this industry between economies of scale and productivity growth rates.

126

Metal Fabricating Industries 14

The metal fabricating industries produce 8.8 per cent of total manufacturing value added. They employ 118,000 employees in 3,900 establishments, with an average of 30 employees per establishment. This group of industries ranks fourteenth in value added per establishment.

Capacity Utilization

Figure 14-1 shows the potential capacity output and the actual value added in each year from 1961 to 1977. The difference between these two indicates the unutilized capacity through time, and, therefore, output forgone in 1971 constant dollars. This figure shows that the metal fabricating industry group reached full capacity output in 1966, managing a gain of 18 per cent in utilization rate after 1961. From 1966 onward this group experienced varying degrees of excess capacity, reaching a low of 80 per cent in 1977. A comparison of the industry's annual rate of change in capacity utilization with that of the sector shows that in the 1960-70 period this industry surpassed the sector by 2.2 per cent per year. In the 1970-77 period the industry's annual rate of change was −1.20 per cent versus −0.34 per cent in the sector. Relative to all other industry groups in the sector, the metal fabricating group had the fourth highest decline in capacity utilization in the 1970s, while in the 1960s it led the sector by its annual rate of increase in utilization. The industry apparently suffered a severe setback in the 1970s and particularly since 1973.

Labour Productivity, Capital Intensity, and Real Earnings

Table 14-1 shows the industry's average performance in labour productivity, capital intensity, and real earnings compared with that in total manufacturing. Average labour productivity in this industry group was equal to the sectoral average during the 1960s but below it in the

127

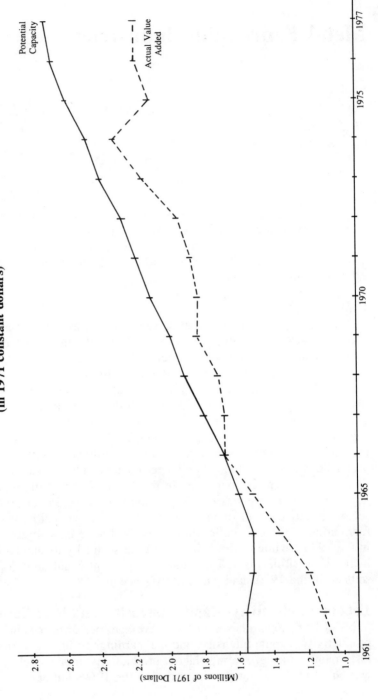

FIGURE 14-1

CAPACITY UTILIZATION, METAL FABRICATING INDUSTRIES

(in 1971 constant dollars)

Potential Capacity

Actual Value Added

(Millions of 1971 Dollars)

128

TABLE 14-1

**AVERAGE ANNUAL PERFORMANCE OF LABOUR PRODUCTIVITY,
CAPITAL INTENSITY, AND REAL EARNINGS,
METAL FABRICATING INDUSTRIES**

	Metal Fabricating	Total Manu.	Industry/ Sector
	(1971 $/hour)		(%)
Labour Productivity			
1960-77	6.17	6.39	96.6
1960-70	5.42	5.34	101.5
1970-77	6.91	7.43	93.0
1973-77	7.15	7.79	91.8
Capital Intensity			
1960-77	4.33	7.89	54.9
1960-70	3.80	6.67	57.0
1970-77	4.86	9.11	53.3
1973-77	4.99	9.53	52.4
Real Earnings			
1960-77	3.49	3.38	103.3
1960-70	3.08	2.96	104.1
1970-77	3.90	3.79	102.9
1973-77	4.05	3.92	103.3

1970s, ranking it eleventh during the 1960s and thirteenth during the 1970-77 period. Average levels of capital intensity in the group were consistently below the sectoral average in all periods, at 57 per cent in the 1960s and 53 per cent in the 1970s. The average level of labour productivity rose 27 per cent from the 1960s to the 1970s. The increase in the average levels of capital intensity for the same periods was 28 per cent, though average capital intensity ranked thirteenth in the sector during the 1960s and tenth during the 1970-77 period. The annual average level of real earnings per hour paid was consistently above the sector average after 1960.

Table 14-2 and Figure 14-2 provide further insight into this industry group's dynamic behaviour. Labour productivity experienced a 1.07 percentage point decline in the annual rate of growth in the industry between the 1960-70 and 1970-77 periods. A significant annual rate of increase in labour productivity occurred in the 1970-73 subperiod (3.98 per cent), while the 1973-77 period produced only a 0.77 per cent annual rate of increase. Throughout all periods this industry's rate

TABLE 14-2

COMPOUNDED ANNUAL RATES OF CHANGE IN LABOUR PRODUCTIVITY, CAPITAL INTENSITY, AND REAL EARNINGS, METAL FABRICATING INDUSTRIES

(% in 1971 constant dollars)

	Metal Fabricating	Total Manu.	Industry/ Sector
Labour Productivity			
1960-77	2.62	3.59	73.0
1960-70	3.20	3.64	87.9
1970-77	2.13	3.53	60.3
1970-73	3.98	5.04	79.0
1973-77	0.77	2.41	32.0
Capital Intensity			
1960-77	1.77	3.00	59.0
1960-70	1.13	2.34	48.3
1970-77	2.40	3.66	65.6
1970-73	2.95	1.90	155.3
1973-77	1.68	5.01	62.4
Real Earnings			
1960-77	2.54	2.63	96.6
1960-70	2.56	2.94	87.1
1970-77	2.51	2.31	108.7
1970-73	2.57	2.72	94.5
1973-77	2.46	2.01	122.4

of growth in productivity was significantly lower than that of the sector, reaching a low of only 32 per cent of the sector's growth rate in 1973-77. There is no doubt that the rates of growth of capacity utilization and those of labour productivity were highly correlated during the post-energy crisis years, but it is hard to establish the exact cause without further research.

The annual rates of growth in capital intensity were not strictly consistent with those of labour productivity (Figure 14-2). In the 1960-77 period, the capital intensity rate of growth fluctuated considerably, declining from 1961 to 1966 and then increasing for the next four years, and averaging an annual rate of growth of 1.13 per cent. During the same decade, labour productivity assumed a smooth rate of growth of 3.2 per cent per year. In the 1970-77 period the annual rate of growth in capital intensity increased from 1.13 per cent

130

FIGURE 14-2
RATES OF CHANGE IN LABOUR PRODUCTIVITY, CAPITAL INTENSITY, REAL EARNINGS, AND ECONOMIES OF SCALE, METAL FABRICATING INDUSTRIES
(in 1971 constant dollars)

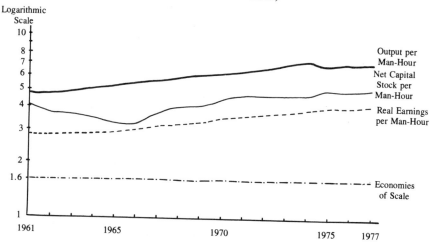

in the 1960s to 2.4 per cent, while the rate of growth in labour productivity declined to 2.13 per cent each year.

The patterns of change in real earnings and labour productivity were not consistent with one another in the various periods either. When the rate of growth in labour productivity declined from the 1960s to the 1970s, the annual rate of growth of real earnings did not change. Compared with the sector's rates of growth in earnings, this industry group changed its position from 13 per cent below the sector rate of growth in the 1960s to 9 per cent above that of the sector in the 1970s.

These relationships are best revealed in Table 14-3, which shows that the annual average of the ratio of labour productivity to real earnings in the industry was 1.77 throughout or that, on average, during this 1961-77 period the level of labour earnings was 57 per cent of the labour productivity level. The ratio of labour productivity to earnings was slightly below the sectoral rate throughout. The rate of progression of the same ratio through time, which is highly relevant to labour and management policy issues, was 1.05 during the whole period. Thus labour received in payments its contribution to productivity growth as expected in production theory. In shorter periods, however, this ideal was violated. In the 1960-70 period labour

131

received only 80 per cent of its contribution to productivity growth, whereas in the 1970-77 period it received 118 per cent of its contribution to productivity growth. The latter simply means that labour received in real purchasing power 18 per cent above what it produced during the 1970s. The fluctuation was, however, violent in the 1970s. In the 1970-73 subperiod labour received only 62 per cent of its contribution to productivity, whereas in the 1973-77 period the metal fabricating industries paid labour in real hourly earnings over threefold (322.6 per cent) of what they produced per hour. While some of this fluctuation could be attributed to random errors in data for these relatively short periods, nevertheless this last wage-productivity relationship is a highly undesirable phenomenon, for gains in purchasing power should always stem from net gains in productivity. If they do not, then inflationary pressures result, as they did in this industry from 1973 to 1977.

Table 14-3 also reveals that the average levels of output-capital

TABLE 14-3

RATIO OF LABOUR PRODUCTIVITY/EARNINGS, OUTPUT/CAPITAL, AND TECHNOLOGICAL CHANGE, METAL FABRICATING INDUSTRIES

(in 1971 constant dollars)

	1960-77	1960-70	1970-77	1970-73	1973-77
AVERAGE LABOUR PRODUCTIVITY/AVERAGE REAL EARNINGS					
Total manufacturing	1.88	1.80	1.96		1.99
Metal Fabricating	1.77	1.76	1.77		1.77
COMPOUNDED RATES OF CHANGE IN LABOUR PRODUCTIVITY/REAL EARNINGS					
Total manufacturing	1.39	1.24	1.53	1.85	1.20
Metal Fabricating	1.05	1.25	0.85	1.62	0.31
AVERAGE OUTPUT/AVERAGE CAPITAL					
Total manufacturing	0.82	0.81	0.82	0.83	0.82
Metal Fabricating	1.43	1.43	1.42	1.42	1.43
COMPOUNDED RATES OF CHANGE IN OUTPUT/CAPITAL					
Total manufacturing	0.57	1.30	−0.16	2.95	−2.43
Metal Fabricating	0.89	2.06	−0.28	2.23	−2.12
COMPOUNDED RATES OF CHANGE IN TECHNOLOGY (%)					
	1960-77	1960-70	1970-77		
Total manufacturing	0.310	0.259	0.361		
Metal Fabricating	0.104	0.361	−0.153		

ratios were 77 per cent higher than those in the sector and were stable throughout the seventeen-year period. However, considerable variation existed in the growth of average productivity of capital. In the 1960s this industry group had a strong annual rate of increase in capital productivity relative to the sector, and it ranked eighth with respect to all other industry groups. But in the 1970-77 period, there was a negative rate of change of 0.28 per cent per year in the industry's capital productivity, mainly because in the 1973-77 subperiod the overall relatively low annual rate of growth in capital productivity (0.89 per cent) constrained total productivity growth in this industry group. To verify this assumption we examined the contribution of technological change to productivity growth.

Estimates of the VES and the CES production functions as well as the Translog production function consistently showed an insignificant contribution of technology to total factor productivity. In addition, all three functions showed a *negative* contribution of technical change to total factor productivity. (See Volume I, Tables 3-10, D-2, D-3 and D-4). Such results imply that the industry not only failed to introduce new technology to enhance its productivity growth, but also experienced a regression in the quality of its plant and equipment.

The strategic question this raises is how the industry has responded (and perhaps would respond) to new technology embodied in its changing stock of capital. One answer emerged from the results of the m variable in the VES production function measuring the impact of technology on labour efficiency. When m equals zero, labour efficiency does not depend on capital; when m is greater than one, technology is productive because capital and labour are highly complementary. The value of m obtained for the metal fabricating industries was 0.84, which ranks eleventh in the sector (Volume I, Table 3-11), and indicates that the introduction of 1 per cent more technology raised labour efficiency 0.84 per cent.

Technological Change, Elasticity of Substitution, Labour Share, and Economies of Scale

The technological progress variable, g, is also derived from the VES production function, giving information on the type of technology used by the industry (or a firm) in its production process. If g assumes a value greater than one, technology is labour using or capital saving; if g is less than one, technology is capital using (or labour saving). Table 14-3 gives the annual rate of growth in technical change during the 1961-77 period. It shows that in the 1960s the industry's rate of change was biased in the direction of labour-using technology at a rate of 0.36 per annum. In the 1970s there was a change in the direction of technology towards capital use, at the rate of 0.15 per year. Figure 14-3 shows clearly the trend and the fluctuations of technological progress in this industry after 1961. It reveals that the industry's technology has all along been slightly more capital using than labour using, with the value of g fluctuating between 0.91 and 0.97. The most significant increase in capital-using technology occurred between 1974 and 1977, at an annual rate of growth of 1.4 per cent. Since g was slightly below one during the whole period, these changes in its value do not imply a radical change in technology from capital-using to labour-intensive practices, but rather marginal changes that were slightly biased towards labour-saving or -using technologies while remaining within the general range of capital-using technology.

The ease with which factors of production can be substituted by one another without reducing total output was estimated, giving the elasticity of substitution of the biased type. The results came from the VES production function, which allows the elasticity of substitution to vary without constraints over time. Figure 14-3 follows the fluctuations of the technical progress variable. Its value in 1961 was 0.79 and up to 1974 it fluctuated very similarly to g, reaching a value of 0.83 in that year. From 1974 to 1977 it decreased by 1.2 per cent per annum, reaching a level of 0.80. When the value of the elasticity of substitution variable is less than one, factors of production are dissimilar and, therefore, not easily substituted without jeopardising total productivity levels. Usually, industries that use capital-intensive technologies possess low values, and this industry tends to lean in this direction.

Figure 14-4 shows the pattern of change in real earnings and that of labour's share of real earnings out of value added. Total payments to labour were a relatively constant 56 per cent from 1964 to 1972; payments to capital were a constant 44 per cent of value added. Real earnings per hour during that period increased from $2.82 to $3.74, or by 2.6 per cent per annum (compounded). Between 1973 and 1977 the share of labour increased from 54 to 58 per cent—that is, by 1.80 per cent per year (compounded)—and real earnings increased by 2.5 per cent per annum. This strengthens our connection between productivity and earnings rates of change. In this industry, labour productivity increased by 0.8 per cent per year during the 1973-77 subperiod, whereas real earnings increased by an annual rate of 2.5 per cent, and capital productivity was negative.

FIGURE 14-3
ELASTICITY OF SUBSTITUTION AND TECHNOLOGICAL CHANGE, METAL FABRICATING INDUSTRIES
(in 1971 constant dollars)

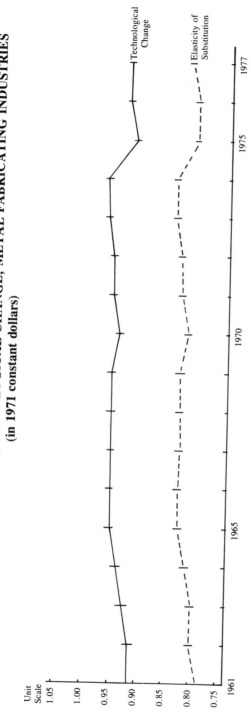

FIGURE 14-4
RATE OF EARNINGS AND LABOUR SHARE OF VALUE ADDED, METAL FABRICATING INDUSTRIES
(in 1971 constant dollars)

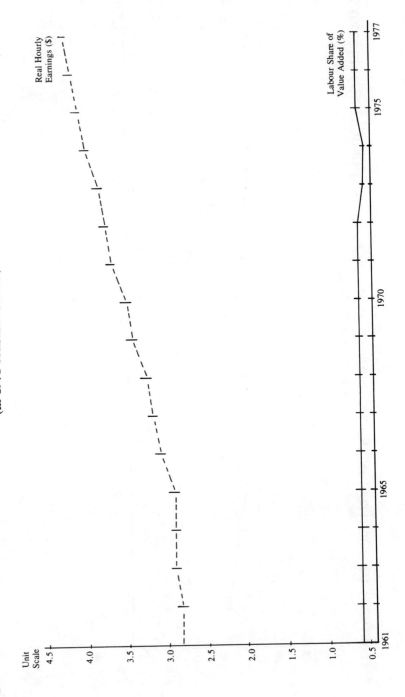

The relationship between productivity performance and economies of scale in this industry was complementary. The metal fabricating industries operated with substantial economies of scale of 1.6 throughout the seventeen-year period and ranked fourth in the sector, while exhibiting relatively mid-sector labour productivity and declining capital productivity. Estimates of the Translog production function show that the economies of scale variable rose at a declining rate and in a statistically insignificant way (Volume I, Table 3-6 and Table D-4), which means that as time progresses, an increase of 1 per cent in inputs would yield smaller than 1.6 per cent returns in output. The Diwan test further identified the contribution of economies of scale to growth in labour productivity as 34 per cent, compared with the 31 per cent average in the sector. These results are somewhat puzzling, because this industry led the sector in the contribution of economies of scale to labour productivity and from the analysis it seems that only scale is contributing to productivity growth; yet that scale advantage was not utilized increasingly through time as capacity utilization decreased continuously.

Machinery Industries

15

The machinery industries group represents 4.7 per cent of total manufacturing value added. It employs about 60,000 people in slightly over 1,000 establishments, with an average of 54 employees per establishment. It ranks eighth in the sector in terms of value added per establishment. The results of this productivity analysis reflect some kind of an average rather than any specific segment within this industry group, since the variety of products of this industry group is quite heterogeneous, ranging from agricultural machinery to office and store machinery.

Capacity Utilization

Figure 15-1 shows this industry's potential capacity output and actual value added real output during the 1961-77 period. The difference between these two indicates the unutilized production capacity throughout that period, and real income forgone. Since optimal allocation of resources occurs only at full capacity operation, labour or capital (or both) are inefficiently utilized in some proportion to the gap of unutilized capacity. The machinery industries group reached its full capacity utilization in 1974. From 1961 to 1966 the utilization rate increased gradually from 67.5 per cent to 90.6 per cent. From 1966 to 1974 there were several fluctuations, falling to low points of 81 and 82 per cent in 1968 and 1971, respectively, and then converging to 100 per cent capacity in 1974. From 1974 to 1977 the capacity utilization rate declined from 100 per cent to 78.6 per cent. Figure 15-1 shows a clear V-shape since 1974, the first indication that this industry was affected by the consequences of the post-energy crisis years; that is, higher capital costs and inflationary pressures affected the demand side of the market. Figure 15-1 reveals that this industry group had relatively large excess capacity for sixteen out of seventeen years of observation. This implies that all along consumers had to pay higher

FIGURE 15-1
CAPACITY UTILIZATION, MACHINERY INDUSTRIES
(in 1971 constant dollars)

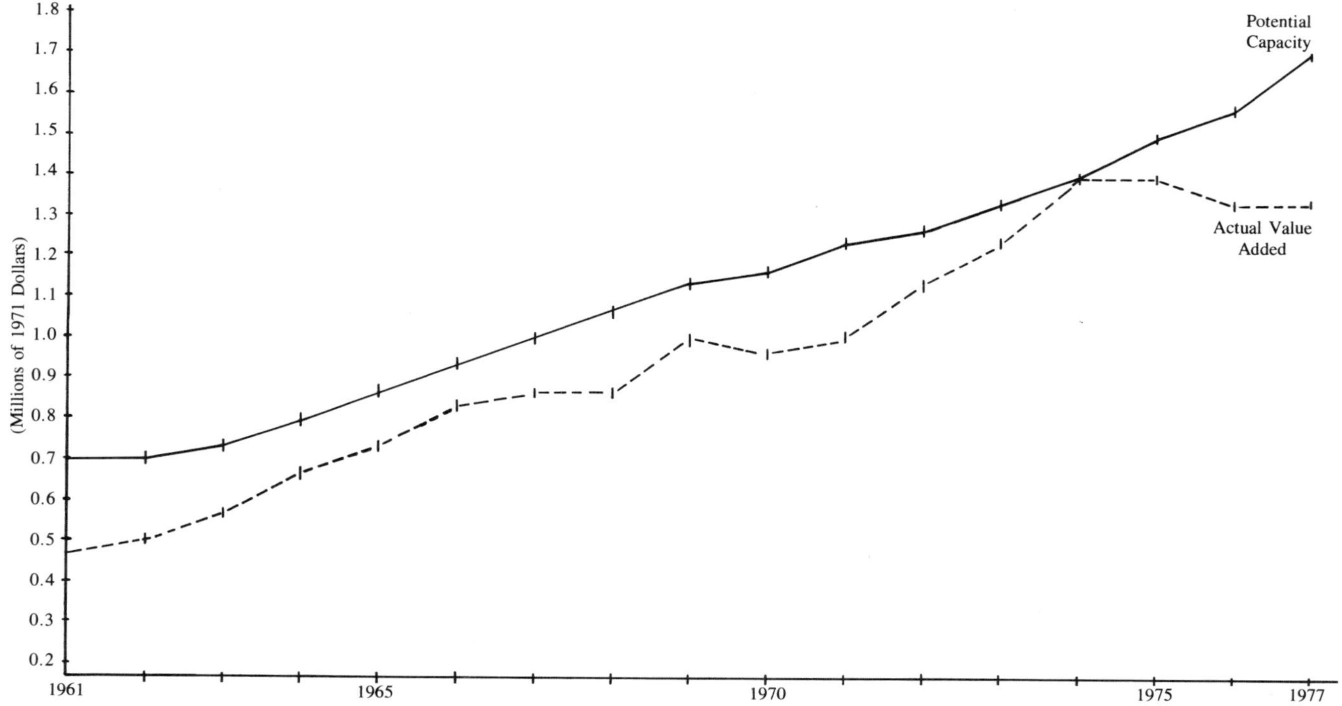

139

prices for the industry's products than they would have if they had operated at or close to their full capacity levels. This factor should be of some concern to both the industry and governments.

A comparison of the industry's annual rate of change in capacity utilization with that of the sector shows that in the 1961-70 period it was 2.36 per cent versus 1.15 per cent. In fact, relative to all other industries in the sector the machinery industries group ranked fourth, a very encouraging phenomenon. In the 1970-77 period the industry experienced an annual rate of decline of 0.83 per cent, which was 2.4 times the rate of decline of the sector. Relative to all other industries, it retreated to a number eleven ranking in the sector. The most severe rate of decline in utilization occurred in this industry in the 1973-77 subperiod, where it led the sector with an annual rate of growth of −4.25 per cent. Because of the nature of the industry's products, demand factors may well influence its capacity utilization rate, since the purchase of durable goods can be postponed and demand for such products is, by and large, relatively elastic. In the period with structural recession and high prices and interest rates, the industry's capacity utilization rates were likely adversely affected.

Labour Productivity, Capital Intensity, and Real Earnings

Table 15-1 compares the industry's average labour productivity, capital intensity, and real earnings with performance in the sector. Average labour productivity in this industry group was between 5 and 7 per cent below the sectoral average. Within the sector, this industry ranked thirteenth during the 1960s and twelfth during the 1970-77 period. The average annual level of real earnings was not consistent with this ranking. In the 1960s the real earnings level was 13 per cent above the sectoral average level; in the 1970s it was 7 per cent higher than the average in the sector. Earnings ranked sixth in the sector in the 1960s and eighth in the 1970s. Average levels of capital intensity in these industries were less than 50 per cent of the sector's between 1960 and 1977, placing them thirteenth in the sector in the 1960s and 1970s.

The compounded rates of annual growth in these three variables demonstrate more encouraging trends. Table 15-2 exhibits these annual rates of change. Labour productivity showed a slight increase in the rate of growth from 1960-70 to 1970-77, while the sector exhibited a slight decrease in the growth rate between these two periods. Consequently, the industry's rates of growth in the 1960s were 93 per cent of the sector's. In the early 1970s the industry outperformed the sector's rates of growth by 46 per cent per annum, but in the 1973-77

TABLE 15-1

AVERAGE ANNUAL PERFORMANCE OF LABOUR PRODUCTIVITY, CAPITAL INTENSITY, AND REAL EARNINGS, MACHINERY INDUSTRIES

	Machinery	Total Manu.	Industry/ Sector
	(1971 $/hour)		(%)
Labour Productivity			
1960-77	6.02	6.39	94.2
1960-70	4.96	5.34	92.9
1970-77	7.07	7.43	95.2
1973-77	7.41	7.79	95.1
Capital Intensity			
1960-77	3.79	7.89	48.0
1960-70	3.30	6.67	49.5
1970-77	4.28	9.11	47.0
1973-77	4.38	9.53	46.0
Real Earnings			
1960-77	3.70	3.38	109.5
1960-70	3.34	2.96	112.8
1970-77	4.06	3.79	107.1
1973-77	4.13	3.92	105.4

subperiod the industry's rate of growth was only 40 per cent of the sector's. Relative to all nineteen industries in the sector, the machinery industries group ranked tenth in terms of annual rate of growth in labour productivity in the 1960s and fifteenth during the 1970-77 period.

The annual rates of growth in real earnings fluctuated entirely differently from those of labour productivity, although according to production theory the rates of change of these two variables should be consistent and the rate of change in the productivity of labour should be the same as that of real earnings by labour. During the 1960-70 period the annual rate of growth in real earnings was 0.6 percentage points slower than that of labour productivity. In the 1970-77 period the annual rate of growth in real earnings declined from 2.79 per cent in the 1960s to 1.41 in the 1970s. The rate of growth in real earnings lagged 2.24 percentage points per year behind the growth in productivity. Although this industry's rates of growth in real earnings were below the sector's in both decades, labour received adequate

TABLE 15-2

COMPOUNDED ANNUAL RATES OF CHANGE IN LABOUR
PRODUCTIVITY, CAPITAL INTENSITY, AND REAL EARNINGS,
MACHINERY INDUSTRIES

(% in 1971 constant dollars)

	Machinery Industries	Total Manu.	Industry/ Sector
Labour Productivity			
1960-77	3.52	3.59	98.1
1960-70	3.39	3.64	93.1
1970-77	3.65	3.53	103.4
1970-73	7.35	5.04	145.8
1973-77	0.96	2.41	39.8
Capital Intensity			
1960-77	2.39	3.00	79.7
1960-70	0.99	2.34	42.3
1970-77	3.79	3.66	103.6
1970-73	4.64	1.90	244.2
1973-77	2.68	5.01	53.5
Real Earnings			
1960-77	2.10	2.63	79.8
1960-70	2.79	2.94	94.9
1970-77	1.41	2.31	61.0
1970-73	0.77	2.72	28.3
1973-77	1.90	2.01	94.5

increases in real earnings relative to its contribution to growth in productivity. This relationship between the change in earnings and productivity is depicted in Figure 15-2.

The annual rate of growth in capital intensity in the 1960s was only 42 per cent of the sector's, while in the 1970s it was 4 per cent above the sector rate of growth. Figure 15-2 shows that capital intensity and labour productivity rates of growth were not similar, and that in 1961-68 and 1971-75 they progressed in opposite directions. The relative position of this industry within the sector, in terms of capital intensity, changed through time. In the 1960s it ranked sixteenth out of the nineteen industry groups, whereas in the 1970s it moved upward to tenth place.

Table 15-3 reveals some interesting information on the relationship between labour productivity and real earnings and about the

FIGURE 15-2

**RATES OF CHANGE IN LABOUR PRODUCTIVITY, CAPITAL
INTENSITY, REAL EARNINGS, AND ECONOMIES OF SCALE,
MACHINERY INDUSTRIES**

(in 1971 constant dollars)

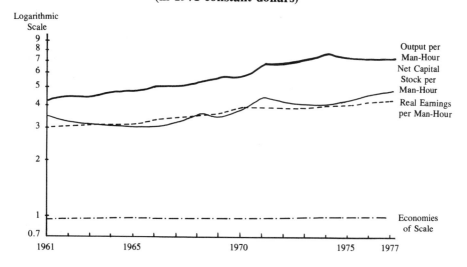

productivity of capital in this industry group. On an average annual
basis, the ratio of labour productivity to real earnings was 1.62 for the
1960s and 1.49 in the 1970s, about 16 per cent and 21 per cent below
the sectoral average respectively. Thus on average, labour received in
real earnings 61.7 per cent of its contribution to productivity growth
during the 1960s and 55.6 per cent during the 1970s. Again, however,
the averages may be misleading, and so we turn to compounded annual
rates of change of the same ratio.

Table 15-3 shows that during the 1960-70 period the annual rate of
increase in real earnings was 82 per cent of the labour contribution to
productivity growth, while in 1970-77 labour received only 38.6 per
cent of its contribution to productivity growth. More specifically, in
the 1970-73 period, labour received 25.8 per cent of productivity
gains; in the 1973-77 period the opposite occurred as the rate of growth
of labour earnings exceeded that of productivity by 196 per cent.
Therefore labour received in real earnings less than its contribution to
productivity growth during most of the period, and total productivity
deficiencies (if any) could only be explained by examining the
productivity of capital and the marginal productivity of capital.

143

TABLE 15-3

RATIO OF LABOUR PRODUCTIVITY/EARNINGS, OUTPUT/CAPITAL, AND TECHNOLOGICAL CHANGE, MACHINERY INDUSTRIES

	1960-77	1960-70	1970-77	1970-73	1973-77
AVERAGE LABOUR PRODUCTIVITY/AVERAGE REAL EARNINGS					
Total manufacturing	1.88	1.80	1.96		1.99
Machinery	1.62	1.49	1.74		1.79
COMPOUNDED RATES OF CHANGE IN LABOUR PRODUCTIVITY/REAL EARNINGS					
Total manufacturing	1.39	1.24	1.53	1.85	1.20
Machinery	1.91	1.22	2.59	3.87	0.51
AVERAGE OUTPUT/AVERAGE CAPITAL					
Total manufacturing	0.81	0.81	0.82	0.83	0.82
Machinery	1.58	1.51	1.65	1.63	1.70
COMPOUNDED RATES OF CHANGE IN OUTPUT/CAPITAL					
Total manufacturing	0.57	1.30	−0.16	2.95	−2.43
Machinery	0.64	2.39	−1.11	4.61	−3.51

COMPOUNDED RATES OF CHANGE IN TECHNOLOGY (%)		
1960-77	1960-70	1970-77
Total manufacturing 0.310	0.259	0.361
Machinery −1.099	−0.664	−1.534

Average figures show that capital productivity throughout was quite high at twice the sectoral average. In the 1960s the annual rates of growth of the contribution of capital to productivity were positive and twice that of the sector. This industry ranked seventh in the sector in terms of average capital productivity. But in the 1970-77 period the growth rate in the productivity of capital was negative and the industry moved into fifteenth place in the sector. In the years before the energy crisis, rate of change in average productivity of capital was extremely high (4.61 per cent per year), which corresponds to the capital intensity "shock" the industry received in the subperiod. In the 1973-77 subperiod the growth rate in average capital productivity was negative, with an annual rate of growth of −3.5 per cent, while capital intensity increased during the same period by an annual rate of 2.7 per cent. Capital productivity, therefore, seems to have been the problem in this industry since 1970.

The question that emerges from these data is whether the quality of capital caused its counter-productivity, or whether the industry was unable to convert the historical rates of growth in capital intensity to a highly productive factor of production. One way to gain some insight into such a complex problem is to measure the impact of technology on labour efficiency, assuming that technology is embodied in capital. Such a measurement is obtained from the VES production function, where m represents the elasticity of labour's response. Our results show that the impact of new technology on labour efficiency during the last two decades assumed an average value of 0.35, which indicates that the productivity of new technology represented by additional capital stock was trivial in this industry: that is, a 1 per cent additional technology resulted in only 0.35 per cent more labour efficiency. The question remains whether a great deal of new technology was introduced into this industry during the period and was not productive or whether little variation in technology occurred in the industry and thus no significant impact was registered. Only an in-depth study of the industry could answer such a question. Our results tend to support the latter possibility, but only tentatively, because a complementary measure from the estimations of the CES and the VES production function clearly shows that the growth in total factor productivity attributable to technological improvement was statistically insignificant throughout the past two decades. These results may imply that improvements in total factor productivity were due to factors other than direct increases in capital stock. Other potential causes are changes in economies of scale and/or other measurements of technological change, to which we now turn.

Economies of Scale, Technological Change, Elasticity of Substitution, and Labour Share

Estimation results of the CES and the Translog production functions show that this industry group enjoyed average economies of scale of 1.01 to 1.06 during the past two decades, so that an additional 1 per cent of factor inputs resulted, on the average, in a 1.03 per cent increase in total output. Computations of the annual rate of change in economies of scale show that the industry experienced a decreasing rate of growth from 0.26 per cent in the 1960s to 0.16 per cent in the 1970s and to -0.08 in the 1973-77 subperiod.

Figure 15-3 shows the technological progress variable, g, of the VES production function, which was greater than the one between 1961 and 1971 and suggests labour-using technology. This variable fluctuated during the 1970s in a declining fashion at an annual rate of -0.7 per cent, starting at a level of 1.24 in 1961 and ending with a value of 1.17 in 1970. Clearly, the technology used in this industry

FIGURE 15-3
ELASTICITY OF SUBSTITUTION AND TECHNOLOGICAL CHANGE, MACHINERY INDUSTRIES
(in 1971 constant dollars)

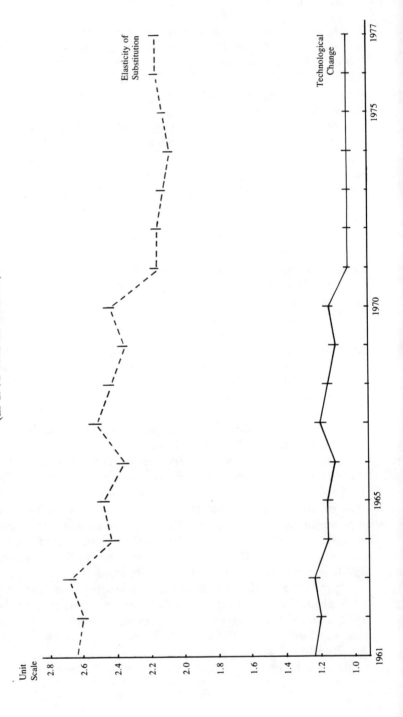

was biased somewhat on the labour-using side. The unprecedented decline in the technological progress function from 1.17 in 1970 to 1.06 in 1971 pinpoints a relatively major injection of capital-using technology in 1971. From 1971 to 1977 there was only a small change of 0.16 per cent per annum, indicating that the industry gradually moved towards less labour-intensive technology, approaching in 1977 an almost "neutral" state of technology.

The ease with which factors of production can be substituted is demonstrated in Figure 15-4, where the elasticity of substitution, in this industry was greater than one throughout; its value in 1961 was 2.65, declining to 2.17 in 1977. This indicates that factors of production can be substituted with relative ease without jeopardising total output.

Figure 15-4 shows the pattern of change in real earnings and in the labour share of value added by the industry. The share of labour declined in this industry from 70 per cent in 1961 to 57 per cent in 1977. Similarly, the share of capital increased from 30 per cent in 1961 to 43 per cent in 1977. The figure compares fluctuations of labour share through time with those in real earnings per hour and shows that real earnings increased at a faster rate when the share of labour showed a more distinct downward trend. In no period since 1961 was there a decrease in real earnings in this industry.

The relationship between economies of scale and productivity is the final area of observation. The machinery industries group experienced economies of scale of 1.01, defined as constant returns to scale situation where a 1 per cent addition to total inputs results in 1 per cent additional output. The annual rates of growth in economies of scale were 0.26 per cent in the 1960s and 0.16 per cent in the 1970s. In the 1973-77 subperiod there was an annual rate of decline of 0.08 per cent in economies of scale. Estimates of the Translog production function show that economies of scale in this industry grew at a declining rate and in a statistically insignificant way, verifying the computations from the CES production functions (Volume I, Tables 3-4 and 3-5). Not surprisingly, the Diwan test showed (Volume I, Table 3-10) that economies of scale had a negative contribution of 9 per cent to growth in labour productivity.

However small, this industry is an important candidate for future expansion because so far most capital goods are imported for Canadian manufacturing, and after paying import tariff the Canadian producer is at a disadvantage compared with his American counterpart. Such expansion, however, would only be economically wise if capital

FIGURE 15-4
RATE OF EARNINGS AND LABOUR SHARE OF VALUE ADDED, MACHINERY INDUSTRIES
(in 1971 constant dollars)

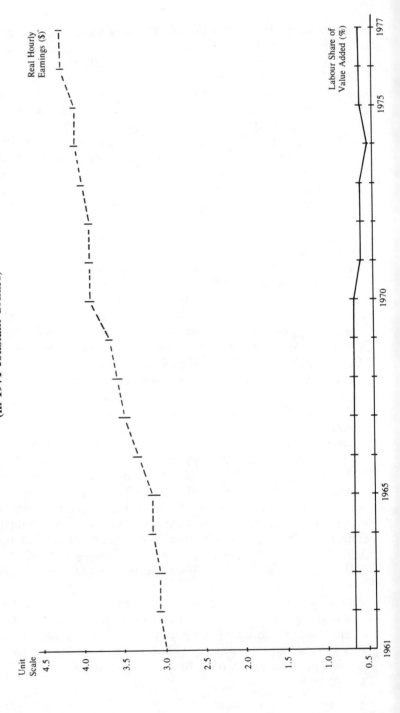

productivity became positive and new technology were introduced into the production processes. Proposals on the type and scope of R & D needed to promote such changes in this industry call for more information than we presently possess.

Transportation Equipment Industries 16

The transportation equipment industry group represents 10.5 per cent of total manufacturing value added, ranking fifth in the sector. It employs 124,000 persons in 970 establishments with an average of 128 employees per establishment. Combining value added and number of employees, this industry group is the second largest in the manufacturing sector. The transportation equipment industry group produces a wide variety of products of which motor vehicles represent 32 per cent of the industry's value added and motor vehicle parts and accessories, 34 per cent. Aircraft and aircraft parts and accessories, shipbuilding and repair, truck bodies and trailers, and railroad rolling stock industry represent 11 per cent, 8 per cent, 9 per cent, and 3 per cent, respectively. This industry group is geographically concentrated in Ontario (84 per cent) and Quebec (9 per cent).

Capacity Utilization

Figure 16-1 shows the industry's potential output and actual value added during the 1946-77 period. The difference between these two curves shows the unutilized potential output or the income forgone. This figure shows that the transportation equipment industry group reached its full capacity output in 1973, after experiencing erratic fluctuations between 1946 and 1953. In 1946 the industry operated at 41 per cent capacity utilization, in 1953 a high of 85 per cent was reached, receding to a low of 50 per cent in 1961, and back to a high of 92 per cent utilization in 1969. In 1975 the industry's capacity to produce was down to 87 per cent and gradually recovered to 95 per cent in 1977.

These kinds of fluctuations in capacity utilization in this particular industry group were not rooted only on the supply side. The variations in utilization reflect changing market demand conditions as well as business cycle fluctuations. Figure 16-1 shows a distinct increase in

150

FIGURE 16-1
CAPACITY UTILIZATION, TRANSPORTATION EQUIPMENT INDUSTRIES
(in 1971 constant dollars)

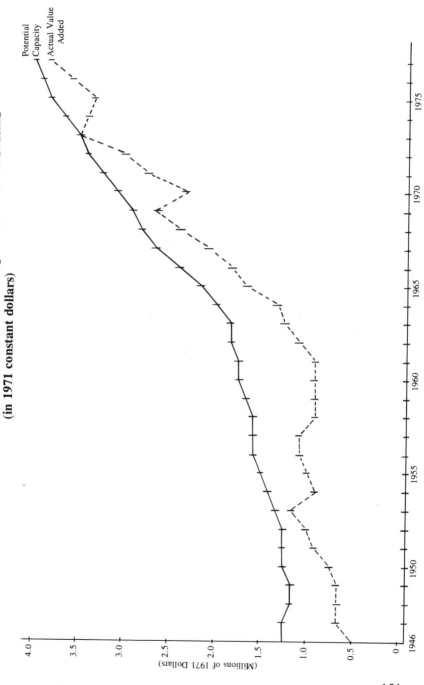

151

capacity utilization since the Canada-U.S. Auto Pact Agreement, when utilization rates increased from the 50 per cent levels to the high 70 per cent levels.

A comparison of the industry's annual rate of growth in capacity utilization with that of the sector's shows that it outperformed the sector's rates of growth in all periods. In the 1960-70 period, the industry increased its capacity utilization by an annual rate of 3.8 per cent, compared with 1.15 per cent in the sector. This was the largest rate of growth within the sector compared with all other industry groups. The main source for this growth was the opening of the U.S. market for Canadian cars and accessories. In the 1970-77 period the annual rate of growth in capacity utilization subsided somewhat to 3.27 per cent, mainly because of the post-energy crisis recessionary trend in the 1973-77 subperiod when the annual rate of growth in utilization was −1.38 per cent.

Labour Productivity, Capital Intensity, and Real Earnings

Table 16-1 compares the industry's average levels of performance in these three variables with those of the sector. Average labour productivity in this industry increased continuously throughout the three decades: in the 1950s it was 6 per cent below the level in total manufacturing, in the 1960s it was 9 per cent above the sectoral average, and in the 1970s it outperformed the sector by 28 per cent. Among average productivity levels in the nineteen industry groups in this sector, this industry ranked ninth in the 1950s and 1960s and fourth in the 1970s.

Average levels of capital intensity in this industry group were always below sectoral average levels. In the 1950s the industry's level was 73 per cent of the sector's, in the 1960s the industry's average was 16 per cent below that of the sector, and in the 1970s it was 21 per cent below the sector average level. Relative to all other industries, this industry group ranked eighth in the 1950s and ninth in the 1960s and 1970s.

The industry's average level of real earnings per hour exceeded the sector average level throughout the three decades by a stable 17 per cent. Relative to all other industries in the sector, this industry group maintained a third place from 1946 to 1970, and declined to a fourth place during the 1970-77 period.

An analysis of average levels of activities of these key variables provides only a partial insight into the industry standing with respect to productivity performance of this industry group. In order to obtain a

TABLE 16-1

AVERAGE ANNUAL PERFORMANCE OF LABOUR PRODUCTIVITY, CAPITAL INTENSITY, AND REAL EARNINGS, TRANSPORTATION EQUIPMENT INDUSTRIES

	Transportation Equipment	Total Manu.	Industry/ Sector
	(1971 $/hour)		(%)
Labour Productivity			
1946-77	5.44	4.93	110.3
1946-60	3.28	3.50	93.7
1960-70	5.80	5.34	108.6
1970-77	9.54	7.43	128.4
1973-77	10.17	7.79	130.6
Capital Intensity			
1946-77	4.83	5.58	86.6
1946-60	3.26	4.47	72.9
1960-70	5.59	6.67	83.8
1970-77	7.13	9.11	78.3
1973-77	7.17	9.53	75.2
Real Earnings			
1946-77	3.22	2.75	117.1
1946-60	2.42	2.07	116.9
1960-70	3.49	2.96	117.9
1970-77	4.42	3.79	116.6
1973-77	4.55	3.92	116.1

complete view of the industry, additional information is necessary about the dynamic changes in these and related variables. Only when we see compounded annual rates of growth can we conclude whether or not the industry has become more or less productive through time and unveil some of the sources for such changes. Table 16-2 and Figure 16-2 are the first two sources for such information.

Table 16-2 shows that the compounded annual rate of growth of labour productivity in this industry group was 3.6 per cent during the 1950s, 7.0 per cent lower than the sector's annual rate of growth in that decade. Within the sector it ranked tenth in terms of productivity. In the 1960s, however, the annual rate of growth in labour productivity doubled in this industry, while that of the sector declined somewhat. In 1960-70, therefore, the rate of change in labour productivity in the industry was twice the sector's, and it experienced the highest rate of growth of all other industries in manufacturing. In the 1970-77 period

153

TABLE 16-2

COMPOUNDED ANNUAL RATES OF CHANGE IN LABOUR PRODUCTIVITY, CAPITAL INTENSITY, AND REAL EARNINGS, TRANSPORTATION EQUIPMENT INDUSTRIES

(% in 1971 constant dollars)

	Transportation Equipment	Total Manu.	Industry/ Sector
Labour Productivity			
1946-77	5.05	3.70	136.5
1946-60	3.57	3.82	93.5
1960-70	7.01	3.64	192.6
1970-77	5.24	3.53	148.4
1970-73	7.44	5.04	147.6
1973-77	3.61	2.41	149.8
Capital Intensity			
1946-77	3.00	3.83	78.3
1946-60	4.05	4.99	81.2
1960-70	3.14	2.34	134.2
1970-77	0.75	3.66	20.5
1970-73	3.77	1.90	198.4
1973-77	−3.13	5.01	
Real Earnings			
1946-77	2.84	2.85	99.6
1946-60	3.04	3.27	93.0
1960-70	2.89	2.94	98.3
1970-77	2.37	2.31	102.6
1970-73	2.57	2.72	94.5
1973-77	2.22	2.01	110.4

their rate of growth in labour productivity was 5.24 per cent per annum, compared with 3.53 per cent in the sector. Relative to all other industry groups in the sector the industry group ranked fifth during that period. When the 1970-77 period is divided into two subperiods, I found that in 1970-73 the annual rate of productivity growth was 7.44 per cent, whereas in 1973-77 it declined to 3.61 per cent per year. In both subperiods the industry's performance was 1.5 times better than the sector's. The industry experienced the highest rate of growth in labour productivity during the 1960s and retreated to the fifth place in the sector in terms of rate of growth in the 1970s. Thus it is interesting to examine whether the source of the slowdown (still, however, among the best five in the sector) can be partly attributed to the rate of growth in capital intensity.

154

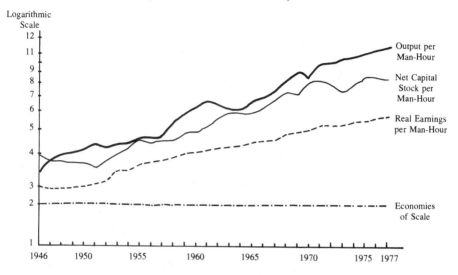

FIGURE 16-2
RATES OF CHANGE IN LABOUR PRODUCTIVITY, CAPITAL
INTENSITY, REAL EARNINGS, AND ECONOMIES OF SCALE,
TRANSPORTATION EQUIPMENT INDUSTRIES
(in 1971 constant dollars)

Table 16-2 shows that the annual rate of growth of capital intensity in the industry was 4.05 per cent during the 1950s, whereas that of the sector was 4.99 per cent. It maintained tenth place in the sector in terms of the capital intensity rate of growth, which was exactly the same ranking as for labour productivity rates of growth in that decade. In the 1960s there was a decline in the industry's annual rate of growth in capital intensity to 3.14 per cent, whereas the decline in the sector dropped to 2.34 per cent per year. Relative to all other industries transportation equipment ranked sixth in that decade, while in terms of productivity rate of change it ranked first in the same period. In 1970-77 there was an unprecedented rate of decline in the rate of growth of capital intensity when it dropped from 3.14 per cent in the 1960s to 0.75 per cent per year in the 1970s. The sector, however, showed an increased annual rate of growth from 2.34 per cent in the 1960s to 3.66 per cent in the 1970s. Relative to all other industries in the sector, this industry group ranked nineteenth, the slowest rate of growth in manufacturing. When the 1970-77 period was divided into two subperiods, I found that in 1970-73 the transportation industries had a 3.77 per cent growth rate, whereas in 1973-77 it had a negative

155

rate of 3.13 per cent per annum. So far we have seen that during the past two decades labour productivity and capital intensity assumed the same direction of annual rates of decline but that the rate of decline in capital intensity was more severe by far. Figure 16-2 provides a view of the relationships in terms of these variables' rates of changes since 1946. Clearly, this figure reveals inconsistencies between changes in labour productivity and capital intensity since 1970.

The annual rates of growth in real earnings per hour paid differed somewhat from those of labour productivity. There was a decline in the rate of growth of earnings in the 1960s, while the labour productivity rate of growth doubled during that decade. In the 1970s, the rate of growth in real earnings continued to decline, but so did labour productivity. In the 1950s and 1960s the rates of growth in real earnings were below those of the sector, whereas in the 1970s they converged. Relative to all other industries in the sector, the transportation equipment industry group ranked eleventh in terms of rates of change in real earnings in the 1950s, ninth in the 1960s, fifteenth in the 1970s, seventeenth in 1970-73, and ninth in 1973-77.

Table 16-3 provides further insight into the relationship between labour productivity and real earnings and examines the productivity of capital and the rate of technological change. The annual average of the ratio of labour productivity to real earnings was below the sectoral average from 1946 to 1970. In the 1970s it exceeded the sector average by 10 per cent. Relative to all other industry groups in the sector, it ranked eleventh in the 1950s, twelfth in the 1960s, and seventh in the 1970s. In sum, average levels of labour productivity exceeded those of real earnings. Averages, however, are inadequate for policy decisions and therefore we proceed to examine the compounded annual rate of change in this ratio.

The rate of change in productivity-earnings ratio reflects changes in the industry's real labour productivity relative to changes in real payments to labour; it also embodies the external effects on the industry of market forces and market structure. In the 1950s this ratio of the rate of change in productivity to that of earnings per hour assumed a value of 1.17, compared with 1.24 in the sector. This means that the rate of growth in real earnings lagged behind the rate of growth in labour productivity by 14 per cent. In the 1960s this industry led the sector in the value of this ratio, which was 2.43. This implies that labour received in real payment 41.2 per cent of its contribution to productivity change. In the 1970s the industry's ratio was 2.21, ranking fourth in the sector, and in this period labour received 45.2 per

156

TABLE 16-3

RATIO OF LABOUR PRODUCTIVITY/EARNINGS, OUTPUT/CAPITAL, AND TECHNOLOGICAL CHANGE, TRANSPORTATION EQUIPMENT INDUSTRIES

(in 1971 constant dollars)

	1946-77	1946-60	1960-70	1970-77	1970-73	1973-77
	AVERAGE LABOUR PRODUCTIVITY/AVERAGE REAL EARNINGS					
Total manufacturing	1.79	1.69	1.80	1.96		1.99
Transportation Equipment	1.69	.36	1.66	2.16		2.24
	COMPOUNDED RATES OF CHANGE IN LABOUR PRODUCTIVITY/REAL EARNINGS					
Total manufacturing	1.30	1.17	1.24	1.53	1.85	1.20
Transportation Equipment	1.78	1.17	2.43	2.21	2.90	1.63
	AVERAGE OUTPUT/AVERAGE CAPITAL					
Total manufacturing	0.81	0.80	0.81	0.82	0.83	0.82
Transportation Equipment	1.12	1.05	1.03	1.34	1.28	1.42
	COMPOUNDED RATES OF CHANGE IN OUTPUT/CAPITAL					
Total manufacturing	−0.14	−1.14	1.30	−0.16	2.95	−2.43
Transportation Equipment	1.98	−0.46	3.74	4.45	10.97	−0.19
	COMPOUNDED RATES OF CHANGE IN TECHNOLOGY (%)					
	1946-77	1960-70	1970-77			
Total manufacturing	0.271	0.259	0.361			
Transportation Equipment	1.269	2.282	0.427			

cent of its contribution to growth in productivity. When the 1970-77 period was divided into two subperiods I found that in 1970-73 labour received 34.5 per cent of its contribution to growth in productivity, and this industry ranked fifth in the sector. In 1973-77, however, labour received 61.3 per cent of its contribution to productivity growth, mainly because of the slowdown in productivity compared with the previous period rather than because of a faster rate of increase in real earnings. In sum, this table shows that this industry group had considerable gains from labour productivity rate of growth, and in this respect it was the second highest in the sector since 1973.

Since this industry was among the highest in the sector in terms of labour productivity rates of growth, and among the lowest in the sector in terms of annual rates of growth in capital intensity, it is interesting to examine its capital productivity and the impact of technology on labour efficiency. The industry's average productivity of capital was 1.05 in the 1950s and improved to 1.34 in the 1970s, compared with 0.81 in the sector and representing mid-sector performance throughout. In the

1950s the annual rate of growth in output-capital ratio was −0.46, compared with −1.14 in the sector. Relative to all other industries, they ranked third. This means that the rate of change in productivity of capital was negative in that decade, but that most other industries experienced higher negative rates of capital productivity in that period. In the 1960s the rate of change in capital productivity was positive and approximately three times that of the sector. Relative to all other industries, this industry group had the second highest rate of growth in capital productivity. In the 1970s, the growth rate of capital productivity increased further to an annual rate of 4.5, compared with −0.16 in the sector. The industry ranked first in the sector in 1970-77. The 1973-77 subperiod showed a negative rate of growth in the productivity of capital of −0.19, compared with −2.43 in the sector, ranking fourth in the sector. I conclude that rate of growth in the productivity of capital has been among the highest in the sector during the past three decades, improving from a third place in the 1950s to a first place in the 1970s. However, since this industry ranks among the lowest in rates of growth in capital intensity, it seems that that is not the source for total productivity growth in this industry.

Evidence from our estimates of the VES production function shows that added capital was insignificant to total productivity growth, and that total factor productivity growth stemming from technological improvements in this industry group during the 1946-77 period was 4.05 per cent, compared with the sectoral average of 2.9 per cent.

A more specific measure derived from the VES production function is the variable m, which is an ex-post quantitative assessment of the impact of technology on labour efficiency. The value of m represents the elasticity of response to a change in technology. The average value obtained for the transportation equipment industry group for the 1946-77 period was 0.32, which placed it sixteenth among the nineteen industry groups in the sector. Thus, on average the impact of technology on labour efficiency was small, so that an additional 1 per cent of the type of technology that has been introduced so far resulted in a 0.32 per cent improvement in labour efficiency—or no radical changes.

Technological Change, Elasticity of Substitution, Labour Share, and Economies of Scale

Figure 16-3 shows that the industry's technical rate of change during the 1950s was in the direction of higher labour use, with g, the technological progress variable, increasing from 0.69 in 1946 to 0.79

158

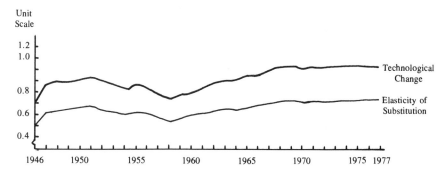

in 1960, an annual rate of growth of 1.3 per cent. In the 1960s the industry group continued to evolve in the same direction, and g increased from 0.79 in 1960 to 0.99 in 1970, an annual rate of growth of 2.3 per cent. In the 1970s there was a significant slowdown in the rate of growth of g to 0.43 per cent per annum, and the absolute value of g was around one. Figure 16-3 shows clearly the rate of change in g through time, which fluctuated considerably from 1946 to 1958, when it hit a trough and increased continuously from that year on.

The variable that shows the degree of ease with which factors of production can be substituted by one another without reducing total output is the elasticity of substitution. Figure 16-3 shows that the two variables are somewhat related. Over the thirty-two-year period, the elasticity of substitution was always less than one, fluctuating almost parallel to g. When g showed a tendency towards labour-using technology, the elasticity of substitution increased and vice versa.

Figure 16-4 shows the pattern of change in real earnings and that in labour of value added of the industry. Labour share fluctuated until 1958, and from that year to 1977 it declined continuously from 82 per cent to 43 per cent; at the same time the share of capital increased from 18 per cent in 1958 to 57 per cent in 1977. Real earnings increased continuously after 1950, giving employees in this industry group a consistent gain in purchasing power. The type of fluctuations shown in Figure 16-4 were typical of contractual wage settlements, in which real wages increased step by step.

The relationship between productivity performance and economies

159

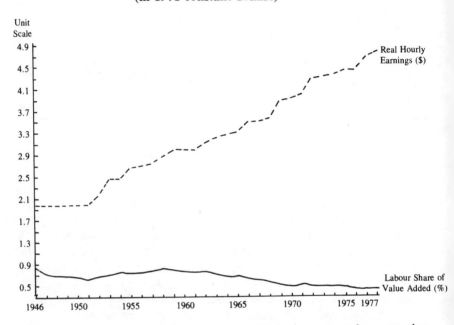

FIGURE 16-4
RATE OF EARNINGS AND LABOUR SHARE OF VALUE ADDED,
TRANSPORTATION EQUIPMENT INDUSTRIES
(in 1971 constant dollars)

of scale in this particular industry group is important because the industry experienced among the highest scale economies throughout the period, ranging from 1.64 to 1.92. The Translog production function also shows clearly that economies of scale were growing at an increasing rate in this industry. This means that as time progresses, a 1 per cent addition to total inputs will result in more than 1.64 or 1.92 per cent in total output. The Diwan test identified the contribution of economies of scale to labour productivity as 25 per cent, the fourth highest in the sector.

160

Electrical and Electronic Products Industries **17**

Capacity Utilization

Figure 17-1 shows that the electrical and electronic products industries experienced excess capacity (of varying degrees) throughout most of the period. They produced at full capacity in 1947 and close to full capacity in 1948, 1955, and 1966. After 1966 the rate of capacity utilization declined from 91.2 per cent to 74.1 per cent in 1974; the annual rate of decline became more acute in 1970. During the 1960-70 period, the industries in this group maintained a compounded rate of annual growth of 1.53 per cent in their capacity utilization. In the 1970s this pattern reversed, with an annual growth rate of −0.54 per cent. In the 1973-77 subperiod the annual rate of growth in capacity utilization accelerated to −2.87 per cent. The figure clearly shows these trends, with an almost V-shaped pattern between potential and actual output since 1973.

Total manufacturing, however, was operating close to full capacity during most of the period, reaching full capacity in 1973. In comparing rates of change, in 1960-70 the sector's annual rate of growth was 0.48 per cent below that of the electrical products industries. After 1970 the annual rate of decline in the industry was greater than that in the manufacturing sector, by about 0.5 to 0.8 per cent per annum.

Labour Productivity and Capital Intensity

Tables 17-1 and 17-2 summarize the industries' performance compared with that in total manufacturing and reveal some notable structural aspects of the electrical products industry. Labour productivity performance in the industry group was slightly below that in the sector throughout the thirty-two-year period, ranging from 93 per cent in the 1950s to almost 98 per cent in the 1970s. The picture for capital intensity was different, since the industries were far less capital

161

FIGURE 17-1
CAPACITY UTILIZATION, ELECTRICAL AND ELECTRONIC PRODUCTS INDUSTRIES
(in 1971 constant dollars)

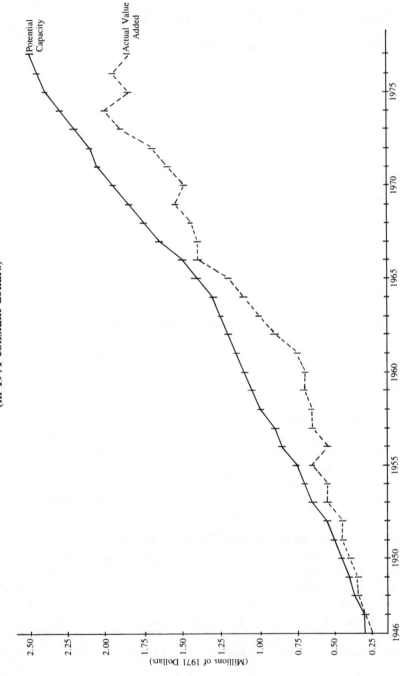

TABLE 17-1

**AVERAGE ANNUAL PERFORMANCE OF LABOUR PRODUCTIVITY,
CAPITAL INTENSITY, AND REAL EARNINGS,
ELECTRICAL AND ELECTRONIC PRODUCTS INDUSTRIES**

	Electrical and Electronic	Total Manu.	Industry/ Sector
	(1971 $/hour)		(%)
Labour Productivity			
1946-77	4.67	4.93	94.7
1946-60	3.26	3.50	93.1
1960-70	5.03	5.34	94.2
1970-77	7.17	7.43	96.5
1973-77	7.62	7.79	97.8
Capital Intensity			
1946-77	2.93	5.58	52.5
1946-60	2.21	4.47	49.4
1960-70	3.09	6.67	46.3
1970-77	4.23	9.11	46.4
1973-77	4.44	9.53	46.6
Real Earnings			
1946-77	2.86	2.75	104.0
1946-60	2.25	2.07	108.7
1960-70	3.07	2.96	103.7
1970-77	3.80	3.79	100.3
1973-77	3.90	3.92	99.5

intensive than the manufacturing sector as a whole. For the whole 1946-77 period, capital intensity amounted to only 52.5 per cent of the sectoral average, while in various periods it fell below the 50 per cent level.

The more interesting and meaningful phenomenon is observed, however, in Table 17-2, where the dynamic behaviour of the industry group is compared with the sector's performance, measured as a compounded annual rate of growth. For the whole period the electrical products industries' annual rate of growth in productivity exceeded the sector's average by 5.7 per cent. But their performance during the 1970s and in particular after 1973 is more startling. The annual rate of change in productivity exceeded the sector's performance in 1970-73 by 7.3 per cent and in 1973-77 by 58.5 per cent. This unusual acceleration in the rate of growth in labour productivity was coupled

TABLE 17-2

**COMPOUNDED ANNUAL RATES OF CHANGE IN LABOUR
PRODUCTIVITY, CAPITAL INTENSITY, REAL EARNINGS AND
TECHNOLOGICAL CHANGE, ELECTRICAL AND ELECTRONIC
PRODUCTS INDUSTRIES**
(% in 1971 constant dollars)

	Electrical and Electronic	Total Manu.	Industry/ Sector
Labour Productivity			
1946-77	3.91	3.70	105.7
1946-60	3.76	3.82	98.4
1960-70	3.71	3.64	101.9
1970-77	4.50	3.53	129.7
1970-73	5.41	5.04	107.3
1973-77	3.82	2.41	158.5
Capital Intensity			
1946-77	4.67	3.83	121.9
1946-60	7.48	4.99	149.9
1960-70	0.87	2.34	37.2
1970-77	4.68	3.66	127.9
1970-73	6.92	1.90	364.2
1973-77	1.75	5.01	34.9
Real Earnings			
1946-77	2.84	2.85	99.6
1946-60	3.55	3.27	108.6
1960-70	2.42	2.94	82.3
1970-77	2.27	2.31	98.3
1970-73	1.22	2.72	44.9
1973-77	3.07	2.01	152.7
Technological Change			
1946-77	0.945	0.263	
1960-70	1.428	0.235	
1970-77	1.326	0.315	

with a sharp increase in the rate of growth in capital intensity during the 1970s. From an extremely low annual rate of growth of 0.87 per cent during the 1960s, the growth of capital intensity accelerated to a rate of 4.68 per cent in 1970-77 and 6.9 per cent in 1970-73. Aside from the 1960-70 decade, the rate of capital intensification in the industry group was above the sector's mark by over 25 per cent. The heaviest capital intensification period was in the 1950s, with a renewed injection in the 1970-73 subperiod.

Increased capital intensity is an indication of technological advances, and increased productivity implies an increase in labour efficiency. It is therefore crucial to measure the impact of changes in technology on labour efficiency. Such a measure is derived from our VES production function in the form of an elasticity of response coefficient, m. Comparing the electrical products industries with the sector, their coefficient was 0.45 and the sector's was 0.40. Although a complementary relationship exists between technological improvement and labour efficiency, it is relatively low, compared with the rest of the sector's industry groups. The interpretation of this coefficient is as follows: an addition of 1 per cent in technical progress (such as highly productive new capital per hour, or implementation of new methods) will result in 0.45 per cent improvement in labour efficiency.

Two more measures of technological change indicate the impact of technological improvement on total factor productivity, both of which are derived and estimated in the VES form. The technological progress function g shows the bias of the technology in the industry, which is either labour or capital intensive: if the value of g is less than one, the industry is capital intensive; if it is above one then the technology production is labour intensive. The more capital intensive the industry is, the more difficult it becomes to substitute labour for capital without altering productivity. This is why we see in Figure 17-3 that the elasticity of substitution variable consistently followed the trend of capital intensity of production technology, and why it is less than one when g is less than one. After 1956 the industry group became less capital intensive and the elasticity of substitution increased in value to exceed one in 1977. A comparative analysis with the sector shows that overall it also, though to a far lesser degree than the electrical products industries, became less capital intensive. The rates of technological change in Table 17-2 point out clearly that the industries' decrease in the rate of growth in capital intensity exceeded the sector's average by several times.

We then turn to measure the percentage contribution to growth in productivity from economies of scale. Here we find that 23 per cent of the growth in productivity in the industries was indeed due to scale of operation. This figure is below the sectoral average of 31 per cent.

These findings are undoubtedly too aggregated, since Statistics Canada includes the electrical and the electronics firms in one industry group, which could be very misleading. Thus our findings represent "average" performance in the industry as defined by official data classification. More conclusive implications could be drawn only if a

165

FIGURE 17-2
RATES OF CHANGE IN LABOUR PRODUCTIVITY, CAPITAL INTENSITY, REAL EARNINGS, AND ECONOMIES OF SCALE, ELECTRICAL AND ELECTRONIC PRODUCTS INDUSTRIES
(in 1971 constant dollars)

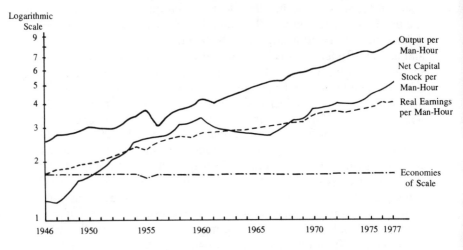

productivity study were to be conducted separately for the electronics industry and the electrical industry.

The relationships between the growth rates of capital intensity and labour productivity in the pre-energy crisis and post-energy crisis subperiods are important. The increase in capital intensity during 1973-77 was "less productive" than in the previous subperiod (1970-73); for example, Table 17-2 shows a 1.75 per cent annual rate of increase in capital intensity compared with a 3.82 per cent annual rate of increase in labour productivity; whereas in the 1970-73 subperiod capital intensity grew at a rate of 6.92 per cent, and productivity at a rate of 5.41 per cent.

Next we turn to the relationship between the rates of increase in real wages and in productivity. Table 17-2 and Figure 17-2 demonstrate clearly that the rate of increase in real wages was well *below* the rate of increase in labour productivity through the thirty-two-year period. This implies net productivity gains to the industry group, indicating efficient management of production. The table, plotted on a logarithmic scale, gives the rates of change. In 1966 capital intensity began to rise at a faster rate than wages, with its rate of increase exceeding that of labour productivity up to 1960 and from 1970 to

166

1977. Economies of scale were stable and above one throughout the whole period. The Translog production function indicated that the industry's economies of scale grew at an increasing rate throughout the period. A striking fact is that this industry enjoyed structural economies of scale of 1.7, meaning that if total factor inputs were increased by 1 per cent, total output would increase by 1.7 per cent.

The process of capital intensification increases the share of capital in the value added. This, by definition, decreases relative payments to labour and, therefore, labour's share in value added is decreased. Figure 17-4 shows that, while real wages per hour increased throughout the period, labour's share decreased noticeably after 1961, with a significant drop after 1971.

Other relationships in this industry deserve attention. Figure 17-3 and Table 17-3 show the results of our analysis of the relation of productivity to real wages and the trend of growth in capital productivity as the industry increased its capital intensity. On the

TABLE 17-3

RATIO OF LABOUR PRODUCTIVITY/EARNINGS, OUTPUT/CAPITAL, AND TECHNOLOGICAL CHANGE, ELECTRICAL AND ELECTRONIC PRODUCTS INDUSTRIES

(in 1971 constant dollars)

	1946-77	1946-60	1960-70	1970-77	1970-73	1973-77
	AVERAGE LABOUR PRODUCTIVITY/AVERAGE REAL EARNINGS					
Total manufacturing	1.79	1.69	1.80	1.96		1.99
Electrical and Electronic	1.63	1.45	1.64	1.89		1.95
	COMPOUNDED RATES OF CHANGE IN LABOUR PRODUCTIVITY/REAL EARNINGS					
Total manufacturing	1.26	1.17	1.24	1.52		1.60
Electrical and Electronic	1.38	1.06	1.65	1.97		1.24
	AVERAGE OUTPUT/AVERAGE CAPITAL					
Total manufacturing	0.13	1.15	−1.27	0.15	−2.998	2.57
Electrical and Electronic	0.73	3.54	−2.73	0.13	−3.504	2.96
	COMPOUNDED RATES OF CHANGE IN OUTPUT/CAPITAL					
Total manufacturing	−0.14	−1.14	1.30	−0.16	2.95	−2.43
Electrical and Electronic	−0.72	−3.46	2.81	−0.14	3.61	−2.87

	COMPOUNDED RATES OF CHANGE IN TECHNOLOGY (%)		
	1946-77	1960-70	1970-77
Total manufacturing	0.271	0.259	0.361
Electrical and Electronic	0.976	1.572	1.517

167

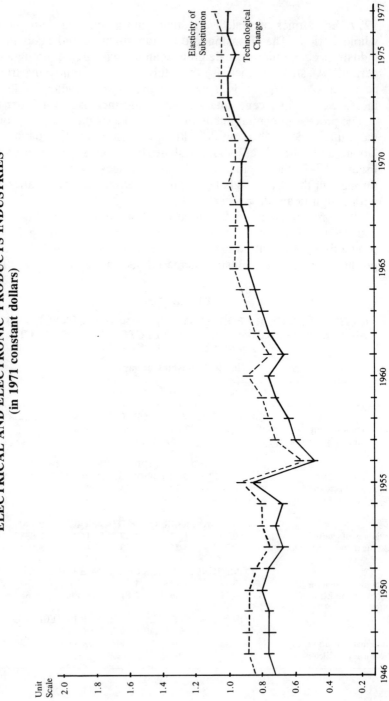

FIGURE 17-3

**ELASTICITY OF SUBSTITUTION AND TECHNOLOGICAL CHANGE,
ELECTRICAL AND ELECTRONIC PRODUCTS INDUSTRIES**

(in 1971 constant dollars)

labour side, the rates of average labour productivity to average real earnings ranged from 1.5 to about 20.0, implying that labour productivity was on the average much higher than real earnings paid to labour. In the 1973-77 subperiod average labour productivity was twice as high as real wages per hour and did not decline as a result of the energy crisis. When the rate of change ratios are derived (marginal ratios), the performance picture alters somewhat. First, the industries' performance moves from below to above the sector's performance. Second, we see a significant marginal increase in labour productivity relative to real wages from the 1950s to the 1960s—0.60 percentage points per annum—and into the 1970s. From 1973 until 1977 this trend reversed and the rate of productivity increase slowed by 0.7 percentage points per annum. In this subperiod the industries experienced a slowdown in the rate of productivity increase from 3.9 to 3.8 per cent per annum, but labour received in real earnings only 50.8 per cent of its contribution to the rate of change in productivity during 1970-77, compared with 80.6 per cent in 1973-77.

What, if not labour, is the source of this decline in total productivity? To answer the question, we need to examine the growth rate of average productivity of capital as capital intensity increases through the periods. Table 17-3 shows that, up to 1970, the trend in the growth of the productivity of capital in the electrical products industries was similar to that in total manufacturing, but that productivity of capital fluctuated more severely in these industries. During the 1946-60 period the decrease in the rate of growth in capital productivity was more pronounced in the industries than in the sector. In the 1960-70 period the industries increased their capital productivity by 6.3 percentage points per annum, compared with the 1946-60 period. The decline in the rate of growth in productivity of capital started in 1970, and the rate of that decrease accelerated to 2.9 per cent per annum during 1973-77—a decline of 5.68 percentage points per annum from the 1960-70 period. The decline in labour productivity for the same periods was less than 0.5 percentage points per annum.

These facts lead to the conclusion that the decline in the productivity of capital should be the prime concern of this industry group and is a potential cause of a further slowdown in the future. Thus it is essential to examine whether the decline in capital productivity is due to the accelerated rate of capital intensity during the last several years or to an excess of obsolete capital still used in production. Industry executives indicated that the latter possibility is a more accurate reflection of the present situation. If this is a valid argument co-operative action by

169

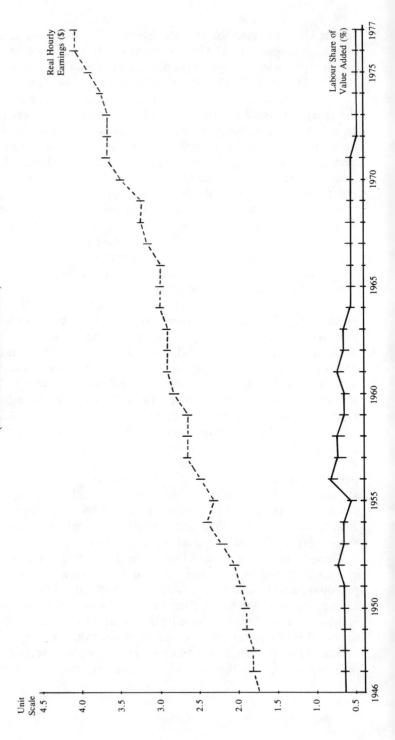

FIGURE 17-4
RATE OF EARNINGS AND LABOUR SHARE OF VALUE ADDED, ELECTRICAL AND ELECTRONIC PRODUCTS INDUSTRIES
(in 1971 constant dollars)

government and business is needed to correct this situation in order to maintain industry competitiveness in the decade ahead. Given these findings, however aggregative, it seems that once capital is made more productive, then labour efficiency will increase at a far faster rate than it has in the past.

Non-Metallic Mineral Products Industries 18

The non-metallic mineral products industries represent 4 per cent of total manufacturing value added, and employed 41,000 workers in 1,182 establishments in 1976 with an average of 35 employees per establishment. This industry group ranked eleventh out of nineteen industries in the sector in terms of value added per establishment.

Within this industry group, concrete products and ready-mix concrete manufactured products were manufactured in 1,050 establishments, which accounted for 89 per cent of the total in the industry; this branch of establishments contained 59 per cent of the value added. The other large group of establishments in this industry group is the glass and glass products manufacturers, which accounted for 32 per cent of the industry's value added. The analysis is dominated by these two segments, which accounted for 91 per cent of the industries' value added.

Capacity Utilization

Figure 18-1 shows the industry's potential output and its value added during the past three decades. The difference, or the gap, between these two indicates the extent of unutilized production capacity throughout the 1946-77 period. The non-metallic mineral products industry group reached its full capacity output in 1965, progressing from 56 per cent capacity utilization in 1946 to 100 per cent in 1965. The two low points within this twenty-year period coincided with the business cycle trough in 1960-61. From 1965 on, the industry had a low of 76 per cent capacity utilization in 1970, a high of 95 per cent in 1973, and ended the series with 88 per cent utilization in 1977.

When compounded annual rates of growth in capacity utilization were examined, the industry group increased its capacity utilization in the 1950s by 2.36 per cent, compared with 0.02 per cent in the sector. In that decade, this group led the sector in annual rate of growth. In the

FIGURE 18-1
CAPACITY UTILIZATION, NON-METALLIC MINERAL PRODUCTS INDUSTRIES
(in 1971 constant dollars)

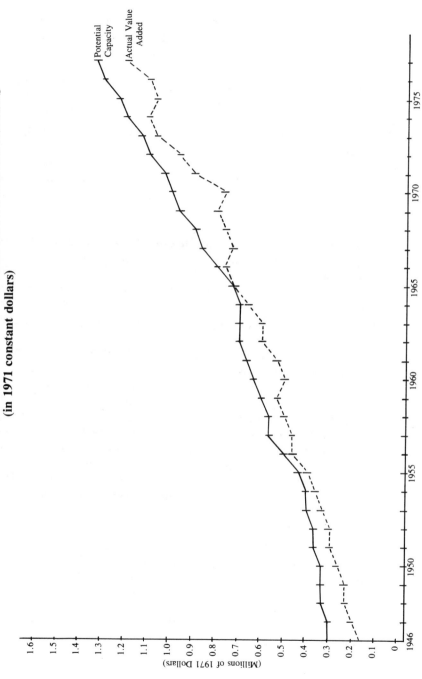

173

1960s, however, this industry group had a negative rate of growth of −0.26 per cent per year, compared with 1.15 per cent in the sector. In that decade this industry group was thirteenth in the sector in its capacity utilization growth rate. In the 1970s it experienced an annual rate of growth of 2.0 per cent in its capacity utilization, compared with −0.34 in the sector, and ranked fourth in the sector. In the 1973-77 subperiod this industry group experienced a negative rate of growth of 1.82, compared with −2.57 in the sector and was ninth, compared with the performance of all other industries in the sector. Because of the nature of the group's products, fluctuations in capacity utilization could be closely related to fluctuations in domestic market demand conditions, in addition to factors on the supply side, which are investigated below.

Labour Productivity, Capital Intensity, and Real Earnings

Table 18-1 shows the industries' annual average performance in these three variables, compared with those in total manufacturing. The non-metallic mineral products industries continuously increased their average annual levels of labour productivity after 1946, and throughout the three decades studied average productivity levels were about 20 per cent above the sectoral average. Relative to all other industries in the sector, they ranked seventh in the 1950s and 1960s and fifth in the 1970-77 period. The industries' average capital intensity levels also increased continuously from one decade to the next and outperformed the sector by 50 per cent, ranking fourth among the industries in the 1950s and fifth in the 1960s and 1970s. Average levels of real earnings also continued to increase from one decade to the next after 1946. However, in terms of this variable, the industries' performance was 4 per cent below the sectoral average level in the 1950s, about the same in the 1960s, and 4 per cent above the sectoral level in the 1970s. They ranked eighth in the 1950s, twelfth in the 1960s, and ninth in the 1970s.

The dynamic changes in these three variables are shown in Table 18-2 where these changes were computed as compounded annual rates of growth for the entire thirty-two-year period and for the various periods. This table shows a 1.92 percentage point annual decline in the industries' rate of growth of labour productivity from the 1946-60 period to the 1960-70 period, compared with 0.18 points decline in the sector's rate of growth. In the 1970-77 period, the industries accelerated their rate of growth in labour productivity to a 6.2 per cent per annum (an increase of 3.5 percentage points), compared with 3.5

174

TABLE 18-1

AVERAGE ANNUAL PERFORMANCE OF LABOUR PRODUCTIVITY,
CAPITAL INTENSITY, AND REAL EARNINGS,
NON-METALLIC MINERAL PRODUCTS INDUSTRIES

	Non-Metallic Mineral	Total Manu.	Industry/ Sector
	(1971 $/hour)		(%)
Labour Productivity			
1946-77	5.91	4.93	119.7
1946-60	4.30	3.50	122.9
1960-70	6.25	5.34	117.0
1970-77	8.86	7.43	119.2
1973-77	9.52	7.79	122.2
Capital Intensity			
1946-77	9.31	5.58	166.8
1946-60	6.82	4.47	152.6
1960-70	10.09	6.67	151.3
1970-77	13.53	9.11	148.5
1973-77	14.08	9.53	147.7
Real Earnings			
1946-77	2.74	2.75	99.6
1946-60	1.99	2.07	96.1
1960-70	2.94	2.96	99.3
1970-77	3.95	3.79	104.2
1973-77	4.15	3.92	105.9

per cent in the sector. Relative to all other industries in the sector this industry group ranked sixth in the 1950s, fifteenth in the 1960s, and second in the 1970s. When the 1970-77 period was divided into two subperiods, we found that the annual rate of growth of labour productivity continued to increase in 1970-73 and was 56 per cent greater than in the sector. In the 1973-77 subperiod there was a decline in the annual rate of growth, but it was still twice the rate in the sector.

The annual rates of growth in real earnings behaved somewhat differently from those of labour productivity. The table also shows that there was a decline of 0.56 percentage points in the annual rate of growth of real earning from the 1950s to the 1960s; the decline in the rate of growth in labour productivity between these two decades was 1.9 percentage points. The real earnings growth rate rose by 0.61 percentage points from the 1960s to the 1970s, whereas the annual rate

TABLE 18-2

COMPOUNDED ANNUAL RATES OF CHANGE IN LABOUR PRODUCTIVITY, CAPITAL INTENSITY, AND REAL EARNINGS, NON-METALLIC MINERAL PRODUCTS INDUSTRIES

(% in 1971 constant dollars)

	Non-Metallic Mineral	Total Manu.	Industry/ Sector
Labour Productivity			
1946-77	4.28	3.70	115.7
1946-60	4.52	3.82	118.3
1960-70	2.64	3.64	72.5
1970-77	6.17	3.53	174.8
1970-73	7.89	5.04	156.5
1973-77	4.89	2.41	202.9
Capital Intensity			
1946-77	3.38	3.83	88.3
1946-60	3.80	4.99	76.2
1960-70	3.00	2.34	128.2
1970-77	3.09	3.66	84.4
1970-73	−0.78	5.01	
1973-77	6.10	1.90	321.1
Real Earnings			
1946-77	3.61	2.85	126.7
1946-60	3.78	3.27	115.6
1960-70	3.22	2.94	109.5
1970-77	3.83	2.31	165.8
1970-73	3.45	2.72	126.8
1973-77	4.11	2.01	204.5

of growth in labour productivity increased 3.5 percentage points. Throughout the thirty-two-year period the rates of growth of real earnings in this industry group were above those of the sector, fluctuating from 10 per cent in the 1960s to twice the sectoral rate from 1973 until 1977. The relationships between the rates of change in labour productivity and those in real earnings in this industry are best viewed in Figure 18-2. Relative to all other industry groups in the sector the non-metallic minerals industries group ranked, in terms of rates of change in real earnings, as follows: fourth in the 1950s and fifth in the 1960s and 1970s.

The annual rates of growth in capital intensity were not strictly consistent with those in labour productivity. The relationship between

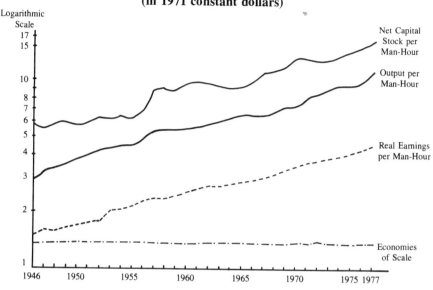

FIGURE 18-2
RATES OF CHANGE IN LABOUR PRODUCTIVITY, CAPITAL
INTENSITY, REAL EARNINGS, AND ECONOMIES OF SCALE,
NON-METALLIC MINERAL PRODUCTS INDUSTRIES
(in 1971 constant dollars)

these two variables is also given in Figure 18-2. In the 1946-60 period the industries' annual rate of growth was 3.8 per cent, compared with 5.0 per cent in the sector. In that decade, they ranked tenth in terms of growth rate. In the 1960-70 period the industries' annual rate of growth declined somewhat to 3.0 per cent per year, whereas that of the sector declined to 2.3 per cent per annum. Relative to other industry groups in the sector, this industry group ranked seventh in the 1960s. In the 1970-77 period the industries' annual rate of growth increased to 3.1 per cent, while that of the sector increased to 3.7 per cent. These industries' relative position in the sector in terms of capital intensity rates of growth was tenth in the 1950s, seventh in the 1960s, and fourteenth in the 1970s.

Table 18-3 gives additional insight into the relations between labour productivity and real earnings, as well as an exposition of the areas of capital productivity and technological change. Average annual levels of the ratio of labour productivity to real earnings fluctuated between 2.13 and 2.24, compared with the sector average levels of 1.69 to 1.96. This means that, on average, during the past three decades the

177

TABLE 18-3

RATIO OF LABOUR PRODUCTIVITY/EARNINGS, OUTPUT/CAPITAL, AND TECHNOLOGICAL CHANGE, NON-METALLIC MINERAL PRODUCTS INDUSTRIES

(in 1971 constant dollars)

	1946-77	1946-60	1960-70	1970-77	1970-73	1973-77
	AVERAGE LABOUR PRODUCTIVITY/AVERAGE REAL EARNINGS					
Total manufacturing	1.79	1.69	1.80	1.96		1.99
Non-Metallic Mineral	2.16	2.16	2.13	2.24		2.29
	COMPOUNDED RATES OF CHANGE IN LABOUR PRODUCTIVITY/REAL EARNINGS					
Total manufacturing	1.30	1.17	1.24	1.53	1.85	1.20
Non-Metallic Mineral	1.19	1.20	0.82	1.61	2.29	1.19
	AVERAGE OUTPUT/AVERAGE CAPITAL					
Total manufacturing	0.81	0.80	0.81	0.82	0.83	0.82
Non-Metallic Mineral	0.66	0.63	0.57	0.65	0.64	0.68
	COMPOUNDED RATES OF CHANGE IN OUTPUT/CAPITAL					
Total manufacturing	−0.14	−1.14	1.30	−0.16	2.95	−2.43
Non-Metallic Mineral	0.86	0.68	−0.36	2.98	8.80	−1.18
	COMPOUNDED RATES OF CHANGE IN TECHNOLOGY					
	1946-77	1960-70	1970-77			
Total manufacturing	0.271	0.259	0.361			
Non-Metallic Mineral	−0.065	0.101	−0.288			

level of labour earnings in this industry group was in the range of 45 to 47 per cent of its productivity level, compared with 51 to 59 per cent of the sectoral average, placing the industry fourth in the sector throughout. The annual rate of growth of the same ratio during the thirty-two-year period was 1.19. This means that labour received 84 per cent of its contribution to productivity when the last three decades are considered as one period.

What really happened during shorter periods is far more meaningful for policy purposes. In the 1950s, the annual rate of labour productivity exceeded that of real earnings; that ratio was 1:1.2, so that labour received 83.3 per cent of its contribution to productivity gains in real earnings. In the 1960s, however, the annual rate of growth (compounded) of real earnings exceeded that of labour productivity. Consequently, labour received in real earnings 122 per cent of its contribution to productivity gains, and excess payments to labour of 22 per cent did not stem from increased productivity. In the 1970-77

178

period, the gains in labour productivity exceeded by far the gains in real earnings, and labour received 62 per cent of its contribution to growth in productivity (the ratio of productivity to earnings was 1:1.61). Dividing that period into two subperiods gave a value of that ratio of 1:2.29 in 1970-73, when labour received 44 per cent of its contribution to increased productivity. In the 1973-77 subperiod, however, labour received 84 per cent of its contribution to productivity growth.

Although this ratio seems to fluctuate "wildly" from one decade to another, we see quite a consistent relationship between returns to labour and changes in productivity; that is, returns to labour by rate of growth in real earnings were lower in years of highest rate of growth of productivity in this industry. The 1960-70 period was an exception, since labour received in real earnings 22.0 per cent more than it contributed to growth in productivity. Since we do not know the price elasticity of demand for these industries' products, it is impossible to say whether payments to labour during the 1960s reduced their profits (in a highly elastic case) or, consumers overpaid for their products to compensate for excess labour earnings (in the case of price inelastic demand).

Next we examine the productivity of the industries' capital stock. The growth in capital productivity was positive overall, but in the 1960s it was −0.36 and in the post-energy crisis period it was −1.18. The rates of growth in labour and capital productivity are consistent. In the 1960s the relative standing of the industry in the sector in terms of labour productivity was fifteenth; its relative standing in the sector in terms of growth rate in capital productivity was sixteenth. The relative position of this industry in the sector in the 1970s was second in terms of both productivity of capital and labour productivity growth rates. In the post-energy crisis years it was sixth in terms of labour productivity and seventh in terms of average productivity of capital, which should induce labour productivity.

Since capital stock represents production technology, it is useful to examine whether technological change in this industry was statistically significant; that is, whether the new capital stock introduced new production technology. Estimates from the production functions show clearly that the average impact of technological improvements on total factor productivity in this industry group, for the whole 1946-77 period, was 1.1 per cent and thus statistically insignificant. The sectoral average for the same period was 2.9 per cent, and relative to all other industries in the sector, this group ranked seventeenth. The results indicate that this industry group maintained much the same technology throughout.

So far the analysis has shown that these industries had the second highest capital productivity performance in the sector after 1970, coming up from fifteenth and sixteenth place, respectively, in the 1960s. It is, therefore, important to measure the degree of their response to the introduction of new technology. The VES production function provides an answer to this question in the form of its variable m, which measures the impact of technology on labour efficiency. The value of m for this industry is the second highest in the sector, 2.13, such that the introduction of 1 per cent additional technology had (and perhaps will have) an impact of 2.13 per cent on labour efficiency.

Technological Change, Elasticity of Substitution, Labour Share, and Economies of Scale

The technological progress variable, g, derived from the VES production function, provides information on the type of technology used by an industry (or a firm) in its production process. Figure 18-3 reveals that the non-metallic minerals industries' technology evolved from neutral (1.0) in 1946-47 to slightly capital using (0.98) in 1977. During most of the thirty-two years, however, g's value was 0.99. Table 18-3 gives the annual rate of growth in technical change during the past three decades, showing a slight change of -0.065 per cent towards capital-using technology during the 1950s, a 0.101 per cent change towards labour-using technology during the 1960s, and a -0.288 per cent annual change towards capital-using technology during the 1970s.

The VES production function also measures the elasticity of

FIGURE 18-3
ELASTICITY OF SUBSTITUTION AND TECHNOLOGICAL CHANGE, NON-METALLIC MINERAL PRODUCTS INDUSTRIES
(in 1971 constant dollars)

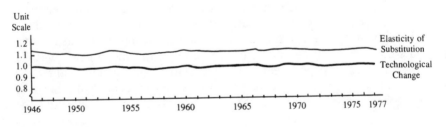

180

substitution of the biased type, giving the degree of ease with which factors of production could be substituted for one another without reducing total output. This variable and g are somewhat consistent with one another as demonstrated in Figure 18-3. Over the thirty-two-year period the values of these industries' elasticity of substitution fluctuated between 1.14 in 1946 to 1.11 in 1977. These values indicate an almost neutral elasticity of substitution, biased somewhat towards a similarity in production factors.

Figure 18-4 shows the pattern of annual changes in real earnings and that of the share of labour real income out of value added. The labour share decreased marginally through the thirty-two-year period from 51 per cent in 1946 to 42 per cent in 1977; however, from 1957 to 1977 it declined by only 2 per cent. Real earnings increased at a greater annual rate in the 1970s than in the previous two decades, but after 1960 real earnings, and thus the real purchasing power of labour in this industry group, increased at an increasing rate of growth.

The last area of investigation is the extent to which economies of

FIGURE 18-4
RATE OF EARNINGS AND LABOUR SHARE OF VALUE ADDED, NON-METALLIC MINERAL PRODUCTS INDUSTRIES
(in 1971 constant dollars)

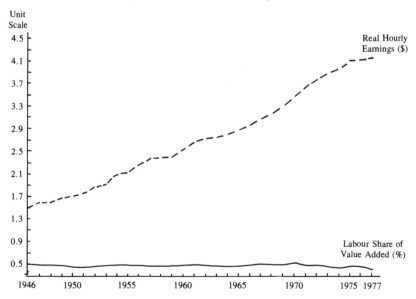

181

scale have or have not contributed to productivity growth. This industry group enjoyed an average level of economies of scale of 1.38 throughout the whole period, as shown in Figure 18-2, such that a 1 per cent increase in factor inputs (capital and labour) resulted in 1.38 per cent increase in total output. An estimate of the Translog production function shows that economies of scale in this group grew significantly and at an increasing rate. If such trend continued into the future, the impact of an increase in total inputs on the resultant increase in output would be even greater. The Diwan test identified the contribution of economies of scale to growth in labour productivity as 24 per cent, compared with 31 per cent in the sector. Relative to all other industries, this was the fifth highest contribution to productivity growth. Therefore, in addition to the marginal productivity of capital, economies of scale played a relatively significant role in enhancing labour productivity in this industry.

Petroleum and Coal Products Industries 19

The petroleum and coal products industries group represents 2.6 per cent of total manufacturing value added. It employed 7,000 persons in 98 establishments, with an average number of 72 employees per establishment in 1976. It ranked second in the manufacturing sector in value added per establishment. This industry group is divided into two main branches: the first is the petroleum refineries branch, consisting of 52 establishments and representing 96 per cent of the industries' value added; the second is the miscellaneous petroleum and coal products branch, containing 46 establishments and representing 4 per cent of the industries' value added. When we disaggregate these two branches in terms of employees and value added output per establishment, the petroleum refining branch shows 264 employees per establishment, and the miscellaneous petroleum and coal products branch shows 33 employees per establishment. In terms of value added per establishment, the first branch ranks first in the sector, whereas the second branch ranks thirteenth. The analysis reflects mainly the performance of the petroleum refineries branch because of its overwhelming dominance of the industry.

Capacity Utilization
Although the computation, or the estimation, of capacity utilization indices involves supply-side variables, such as capital and output of labour, the resulting utilization indices reflect indirectly the market structure in which the industry operates and fluctuations in market demand, both domestically and internationally, for the products in question. In the case of petroleum products, the concentration of the market structure and demand fluctuations influenced capacity utilization fluctuations perhaps more than in any other industry since the early 1970s. In order to exhaust the cause and effect relations of capacity utilization patterns, a demand side study for the industries'

products should be conducted. This is, however, beyond the scope of my present research, and thus, I concentrate primarily on the supply side while only mentioning demand factors.

Figure 19-1 illustrates the industries' potential and actual output during the past two decades. The gap between these two indicates output and therefore income forgone as a result of their inability to utilize full capacity production levels throughout the period. These industries reached their full capacity utilization in 1946 and fluctuations after 1946 did not follow a stable pattern. From 1946 to 1956 actual output fluctuated above the 90 per cent utilization level, except in 1954 and 1955 when utilization rates were in the high 80 per cent levels. From 1957 to 1962 capacity utilization in these industries was in the range of 80 to 86 per cent, with a low of 80 per cent in 1960 and a high of 90 per cent in 1963. From 1964 to 1968 capacity utilization rates fluctuated from 89.5 per cent in 1964 to 95.2 per cent in 1968. A decline in the utilization rate started in 1969, dropping from 94.2 per cent in that year to 89.4 per cent in 1972. These industries experienced a sudden increase in capacity utilization in 1973, reaching the 95 per cent level. From 1974 to 1977 utilization declined continuously from 90.4 per cent to 80.6 per cent in 1977.

The compounded annual rate of growth in capacity utilization indicates more clearly the pattern of fluctuations over the last three decades. In the 1950s, there was an annual rate of decline of 1.54 per cent in this industry group's capacity utilization, compared with the sector's rate of increase of 0.02 per cent per annum. In the 1960s the group's utilization rate increased by 1.17 per cent per year, compared with 1.15 per cent in the sector. Relative to all other industries in the sector this industry group ranked eleventh in terms of utilization rates of growth. In the 1970-77 period there was an annual rate of decline of 1.63 per cent in the petroleum group's capacity utilization, compared with a 0.34 per cent fall in the sector. In that period, the industry group was sixteenth in the sector in terms of capacity rate of decline (negative rate of growth). The post-energy crisis subperiod of 1973-77 showed a far greater negative annual rate of growth (-4.03) in capacity utilization for the petroleum and coal products industries. The sector's rate of negative growth was 2.57 per cent per year. Relative to all other industries in the sector, this industry group maintained its sixteenth place (out of nineteen). This phenomenon is somewhat puzzling at first, for one would have thought that in the post-energy crisis years, when shortages of refinery products were announced continually, the industry would have operated at its full capacity utilization rate or very

FIGURE 19-1

CAPACITY UTILIZATION, PETROLEUM AND COAL PRODUCTS INDUSTRIES

(in 1971 constant dollars)

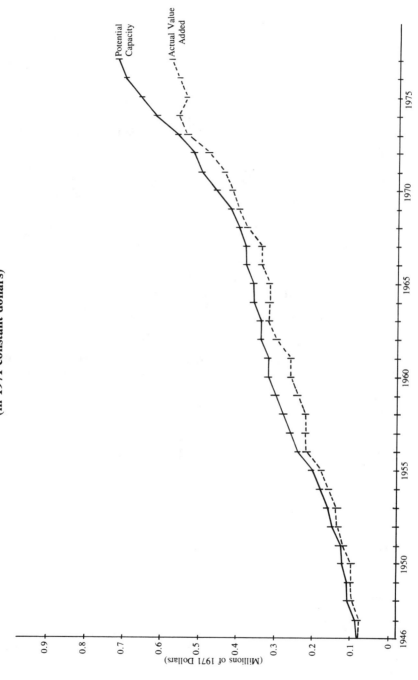

185

close to it. We shall return to this problem when capital productivity is discussed.

Labour and Capital Productivity, Capital Intensity, and Real Earnings

In order to provide a complete picture of the industries' productivity performance, we start with average levels of these three variables and continue with an analysis of their compounded annual rates of growth. Table 19-1 shows the industries' labour productivity performance continuously increased from one decade to the next and was between 70 and 93 per cent higher than the average sectoral levels. Relative to all other industry groups in the sector, petroleum and coal products ranked third in the 1950s, first in the 1960s and 1970s, and second in the 1973-77 subperiod. The average levels of capital intensity of this industry group were the highest in the manufacturing sector throughout

TABLE 19-1

AVERAGE ANNUAL PERFORMANCE OF LABOUR PRODUCTIVITY,
CAPITAL INTENSITY, AND REAL EARNINGS,
PETROLEUM AND COAL PRODUCTS INDUSTRIES

	Petroleum and Coal	Total Manu.	Industry/ Sector
	(1971 $/hour)		(%)
Labour Productivity			
1946-77	8.41	4.93	170.6
1946-60	4.72	3.50	134.9
1960-70	9.87	5.34	184.8
1970-77	14.23	7.43	191.5
1973-77	15.03	7.79	192.9
Capital Intensity			
1946-77	39.81	5.58	713.4
1946-60	23.28	4.47	520.8
1960-70	45.52	6.67	682.5
1970-77	57.33	9.11	629.3
1973-77	72.48	9.53	760.5
Real Earnings			
1946-77	3.81	2.75	138.5
1946-60	2.74	2.07	132.4
1960-70	4.16	2.96	140.5
1970-77	5.46	3.79	144.1
1973-77	5.71	3.92	145.7

186

the two decades. Average annual levels of real earnings were also the highest in the sector throughout.

Table 19-2 and Figure 19-2 help to examine the dynamics of the industry in terms of compounded annual rates of change in the same three variables. The table shows that the annual rate of growth in labour productivity in this industry group fluctuated considerably from one period to the next. In the 1950s it enjoyed an annual rate of growth of 8.3 per cent, compared with 3.8 per cent in the sector. In that decade this industry group experienced the highest annual rate of growth in the manufacturing sector. In the 1960-70 period, the petroleum group's annual rate of growth in labour productivity declined by more than 50 per cent and was 3.72 per cent per year, compared with 3.64 per cent

TABLE 19-2

COMPOUNDED ANNUAL RATES OF CHANGE IN LABOUR PRODUCTIVITY, CAPITAL INTENSITY, AND REAL EARNINGS, PETROLEUM AND COAL PRODUCTS INDUSTRIES

(% in 1971 constant dollars)

	Petroleum and Coal	Total Manu.	Industry/ Sector
Labour Productivity			
1946-77	5.73	3.70	154.9
1946-60	8.30	3.82	217.3
1960-70	3.72	3.64	102.2
1970-77	3.56	3.53	100.8
1970-73	7.48	5.04	148.4
1973-77	0.72	2.41	29.9
Capital Intensity			
1946-77	7.39	3.83	193.0
1946-60	12.95	4.99	295.5
1960-70	1.18	2.34	50.4
1970-77	5.70	3.66	155.7
1970-73	6.39	1.90	336.3
1973-77	5.19	5.01	103.6
Real Earnings			
1946-77	3.61	2.85	126.7
1946-60	4.37	3.27	133.6
1960-70	2.63	2.94	89.5
1970-77	3.53	2.31	152.8
1970-73	2.44	2.72	89.7
1973-77	4.35	2.01	216.4

FIGURE 19-2
RATES OF CHANGE IN LABOUR PRODUCTIVITY, CAPITAL
INTENSITY, REAL EARNINGS, AND ECONOMIES OF SCALE,
PETROLEUM AND COAL PRODUCTS INDUSTRIES
(in 1971 constant dollars)

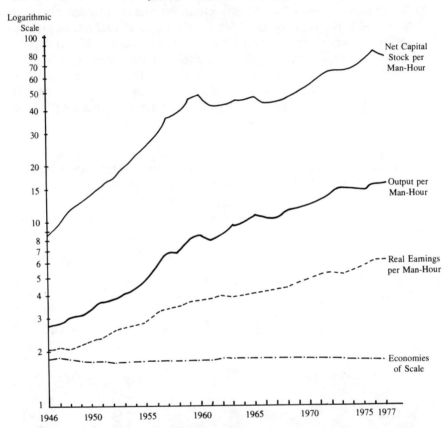

in the sector. The relative position of this group in the sector, in terms of labour productivity growth, retreated from the first place in the 1950s to sixth place in the 1960s. In the 1970-77 period the annual rate of growth in labour productivity continued to deteriorate and was equal to the sector average of 3.56 per cent per annum. Relative to all other industries in the sector, this group ranked sixteenth.

It is of particular interest to examine the rates of productivity growth in the 1970s, prior to the energy crisis and following it. We found that in the 1970-73 subperiod the industries' rate of growth in labour

188

productivity was 7.5 per cent, which was the third highest in the sector. In the 1973-77 subperiod, however, the annual rate of growth in labour productivity was 0.72 per cent, compared with 2.41 per cent in the sector. This weak performance placed these industries in eighteenth place out of nineteen industry groups in the manufacturing sector.

Our next step is to verify whether or not these fluctuations in the rates of growth of labour productivity were related to corresponding changes in the rates of growth in capital intensity. In the 1950s the industries' annual rate of growth in capital intensity was 13 per cent, compared with 5 per cent in the sector, placing the industries in the first place in the sector in this variable. In the 1960s the industries' annual rate of growth in capital intensity dropped to 1.2 per cent per year, compared with 2.3 per cent in the sector. This slowdown in the rate of growth ranked the industry group fourteenth in terms of annual change in capital intensity. In the 1970-77 period, this group's rate of growth increased to 5.7 per cent per year, compared with 3.7 per cent in the sector. Relative to all other industries in the sector, it ranked third in terms of capital intensity rate of growth. In the 1970-73 subperiod its rate of growth in capital intensity was 6.4 per cent per year, compared with 1.9 per cent in the sector, the highest in the sector. In the 1973-77 subperiod the group's annual rate of growth in capital intensity increased to 5.2 per cent, compared with 5.0 per cent in the sector. Relative to all other industries in the sector, it ranked eleventh in this subperiod. A clearcut correspondence between rates of change in labour productivity and capital intensity cannot therefore be established in this industry between 1946 and 1973, although from 1973-77 such correspondence seems to emerge. Nor does Figure 19-2 show a strictly consistent relationship between labour productivity and capital intensity between 1946 and 1973.

The annual rates of growth in hourly real earnings should, according to theory, fluctuate consistently with those of labour productivity. This was not the case in these industries, as is apparent from Figure 19-2. Table 19-2 shows that the annual rate of growth in labour productivity declined by 4.6 percentage points per year from the 1950s to the 1960s, whereas the rate of growth in real earnings declined by 1.7 percentage points. The changes in the annual rates of growth from the 1960s to the 1970s were in the opposite direction. That of real earnings increased by 0.9 percentage points per annum, whereas that of labour productivity declined by 0.2 percentage points. This pattern held for the 1970-73 and 1973-77 subperiods. While the rate of growth of

189

labour productivity decreased annually by 6.8 percentage points, that of real earnings increased by 1.9 percentage points per year.

The relationship between these two variables is important because it leads us to answer whether labour received its contribution to the rate of change in productivity in real earnings or whether returns to labour were below or greater than its contribution to the rate of growth in productivity. Table 19-3 reveals that in the 1950s and in the 1970s labour received in real earnings 53 per cent of its contribution to growth in productivity; and in the 1960s it received 71 per cent. In the 1970-77 period, labour received exactly its marginal contribution to productivity growth, which is a textbook example. In the 1970-73 subperiod, however, labour received only 33 per cent of its contribution to productivity growth. But in the 1973-77 period labour received in real earnings 5.88 times its contribution to productivity growth, an alarming rate because real earnings in this industry during

TABLE 19-3

RATIO OF LABOUR PRODUCTIVITY/EARNINGS, OUTPUT/CAPITAL, AND TECHNOLOGICAL CHANGE, PETROLEUM AND COAL PRODUCTS INDUSTRIES

(in 1971 constant dollars)

	1946-77	1946-60	1960-70	1970-77	1970-73	1973-77
	AVERAGE LABOUR PRODUCTIVITY/AVERAGE REAL EARNING					
Total manufacturing	1.79	1.69	1.80	1.96		1.99
Petroleum and Coal	1.29	1.72	2.73	2.61		2.63
	COMPOUNDED RATES OF CHANGE					
	IN LABOUR PRODUCTIVITY/REAL EARNINGS					
Total manufacturing	1.30	1.17	1.24	1.53	1.85	1.20
Petroleum and Coal	1.59	1.90	1.41	1.01	3.07	0.17
	1960-77	1960-70	1970-77	1970-73	1973-77	
	AVERAGE OUTPUT/AVERAGE CAPITAL					
Total manufacturing	0.82	0.81	0.82	0.83	0.82	
Petroleum and Coal	0.22	0.22	0.21	0.22	0.21	
	COMPOUNDED RATES OF CHANGE IN OUTPUT/CAPITAL					
Total manufacturing	0.42	1.30	−0.16	2.95	−2.43	
Petroleum and Coal	−0.69	2.47	−2.01	1.02	−4.23	
	COMPOUNDED RATES OF CHANGE IN TECHNOLOGY					
	1960-77	1960-70	1970-77			
Total manufacturing	0.310	0.259	0.361			
Petroleum and Coal	−0.933	−1.866	0			

the post-energy crisis years increased 5.9 times faster than labour productivity. Since the price elasticity of demand for refinery products is conceived to be highly inelastic, consumers absorbed most of this real earnings increase by paying higher prices for petroleum products. In this case government intervention is vital to prevent the continuation of such trend.

Since we failed to establish fluctuations in capital intensity as a source for productivity slowdown in this industry between 1946 and 1973, we turn now to examine the productivity of capital as a probable source. Table 19-3 shows that the average level of capital productivity was one-fourth of the sectoral average throughout the last two decades. The more serious point of concern, however, is apparently negative rate of growth in average productivity of capital in the 1970-77 period.

In the 1960-70 period the rate of change in productivity of capital was positive and twice that of the sector. It was the fourth highest capital productivity performance in the manufacturing sector. During that decade, however, this industry ranked sixth in the annual rate of growth in labour productivity. In the 1970-77 period the annual rate of growth in capital productivity was negative (-2.47 per cent) as it was in the sector (-0.16 per cent). Compared with all other industries in the sector, this industry group ranked eighteenth, while in terms of rate of growth in labour productivity it ranked sixteenth. In the 1970-73 subperiod the petroleum group's average productivity of capital increased at a rate of 1.02 per cent, which placed it thirteenth in the sector in terms of this variable. The growth rate of labour productivity was much higher, and placed the industry in the third position in the sector. In the post-energy crisis era, however, the industry experienced a negative rate of growth of 4.2 per cent per year in capital productivity, compared with -2.4 per cent in the sector. Relative to all other industries in the sector it ranked eighteenth in terms of rate of growth in capital productivity, while for the same period this industry group ranked eighteenth in terms of rate of growth in labour productivity.

So far, there seems to be a stronger relationship between changes in the productivity of capital and those of labour than there has been between changes in capital intensity and those of labour productivity from 1946 to 1973. From 1973 to 1977, however, these three variables fluctuated in the same general direction. In the 1970-73 subperiod the relationship between the rates of change in capital intensity and labour productivity were much clearer than between the rates of change in capital productivity and labour productivity.

The negative rate of growth in the average productivity of capital in the 1970s appears to be a serious problem in this industry, particularly after 1973. The question then is whether it is the quality of capital that caused it to be counter-productive and caused labour productivity to decline or whether the low rate of capital utilization in the 1970s caused it to have such low productivity in 1970-73 and to be counter-productive in 1973-77.

Some insight into the problem was gained by measuring the impact of technology on labour efficiency through m in the VES production function, which represents the elasticity of labour's response to technology. The estimates of the VES production function show that the growth in total factor productivity attributable to technological improvements in this industry group was, on average, 8.3 per cent, compared with 2.9 per cent in the sector. Our results also showed that the average impact of technology on labour efficiency during the last two decades was 1.2, indicating that productivity of new technology embodied in added capital stock enhanced labour efficiency in this industry. Since the productivity of capital was very high in the 1960s and very low and negative in the two subperiods in the 1970s, the negativity in 1973-77 was suppressed in the average. Although complementarity between capital and labour efficiency existed, on average, throughout, it is clear that an entirely new and undesirable relation began in 1973. Only a thorough study of the industry could shed more light on this problem.

Economies of Scale, Technological Change, Elasticity of Substitution, and Labour Share

Estimation results of the CES and the Translog production functions show that this industry group enjoyed economies of scale of 1.85 to 1.94 during the past two decades, or that an additional 1 per cent of factor inputs resulted, on average, in a 1.9 per cent increase in total output. Estimates from the Translog production function show that economies of scale were growing at a decreasing rate in a highly significant way, and the CES production function confirms the results. Figure 19-2 shows clearly that economies of scale in this industry group were declining, and Table 19-3 shows a decline from 18.2 in 1946 to 1.79 in 1977. In the light of the economy's future energy needs, this trend is undesirable and cause for future concern in the industry and for the economy.

Figure 19-3 shows the technological progress variable g of the VES production function, which provides information on the type and

192

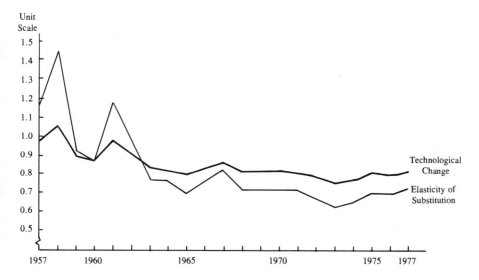

direction of technology implemented by the industry in its production process. The value of g was smaller than one and decreasing from 1957 to 1973 from a value of 0.98 to 0.76, increasing to a value of 0.82 in 1977. This trend implies capital-using technology prevailed in the industry all along. Table 19-3 gives the compounded annual rates of growth in g: in the 1960s the industry group progressed at an annual rate of 1.9 per cent in the direction of capital-using technology; in the 1970-77 period there was no change. When the 1973-77 subperiod was computed, it shows a 1.9 per cent rate of change per year in the direction of labour-using technology, whereas 1970-73 shows an annual rate of change of 2.5 per cent in the direction of capital-using technology. Because of the shortness of these two subperiods there is a high probability of rather large random error, so these annual rates of change are likely to be biased. The direction of technological change seems to be correct since all other computations in previous tables point to the same phenomenon.

The ease with which factors of production can be substituted by one another (within a given technology) without reducing total output is estimated via the VES production function, and the variable which

193

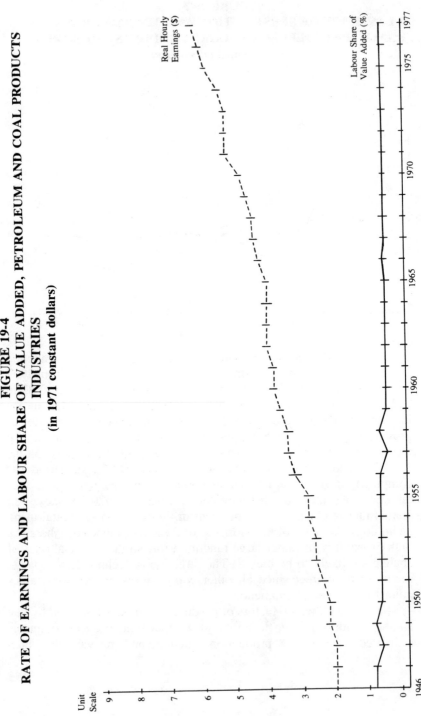

FIGURE 19-4

RATE OF EARNINGS AND LABOUR SHARE OF VALUE ADDED, PETROLEUM AND COAL PRODUCTS INDUSTRIES

(in 1971 constant dollars)

represents the degree of such ease is the variable elasticity of substitution. This variable demonstrated considerable fluctuation between 1957 and 1962 (Figure 19-3). Since this variable is very sensitive to changes in capital stock, these fluctuations were a direct statistical result of the significant drop in the rate of change in capital during that period (see Table 19-2), but the economic meaning of such fluctuations is not clear, since g shows there was no significant change in the technology of production. From 1962 to 1977 the rates of change in the two variables are consistent.

Figure 19-4 shows the rates of change in real earnings and labour share of value added. Real earnings in this industry increased continuously from $2.04 per hour in 1946 to $6.13 per hour in 1977, without a decline in real purchasing power at any given year throughout the thirty-two-year period. The share of labour declined continuously as well throughout, from 58 per cent in 1946 to 38 per cent in 1977; concomitantly, the capital share of value added increased from 42 per cent in 1946 to 62 per cent in 1977, results that are perfectly consistent with the progression towards capital-using technology.

Chemical and Chemical Products Industries

20

The chemical and chemical products industry group represents 6.7 per cent of total manufacturing value added. It employed 43,000 persons in 1,000 establishments in 1976 with an average of 43 employees each. It ranked seventh in the sector in terms of value added per establishment. Since the range of products included in the definition of this industry group is highly diversified—industrial chemicals comprises about 51 per cent and pharmaceutical and medicine products are 17 per cent of this industry's value added output—the results of this productivity analysis cannot be taken as an average performance of the whole group, for they will be somewhat biased by the heavier weighting of these two product groups. This industry group is concentrated primarily in Ontario and Quebec, where the implications of the analysis mainly apply.

Capacity Utilization

Figure 20-1 shows the potential and actual value added output during the 1946-77 period. The gap between these two curves shows the unutilized production capacity and therefore represents the forgone output. The chemical and chemical products industry group reached full capacity output in 1973-74. From 1946 to 1961 capacity utilization fluctuated between 72 and 76 per cent. The industry operated at around 90 per cent capacity utilization between 1964 and 1972 and its utilization rate declined gradually from 86 per cent to 78 per cent in the 1974-77 period. By and large, this industry group has been operating fairly close to capacity compared with most industries in the manufacturing sector. A comparison of annual rates of change in capacity utilization reveals that during the 1960s capacity in the group grew 1.8 per cent compared with 1.2 per cent in the sector. Relative to all other industries in the sector, this one ranked seventh in terms of capacity rate of growth in that period. In the 1970-77 period there was

196

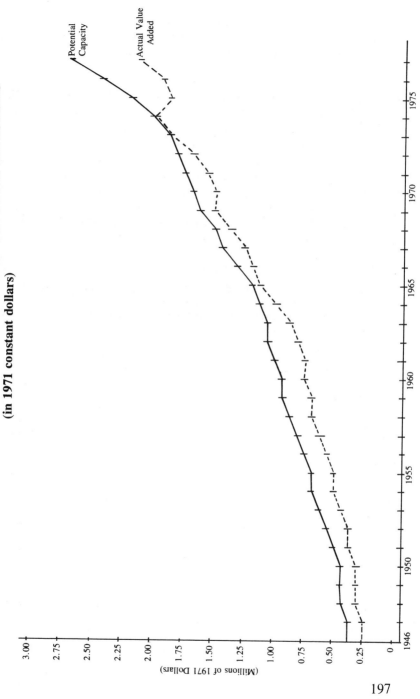

FIGURE 20-1

CAPACITY UTILIZATION, CHEMICAL AND CHEMICAL PRODUCTS INDUSTRIES

(in 1971 constant dollars)

Potential Capacity

Actual Value Added

3.00
2.75
2.50
2.25
2.00
1.75
1.50
1.25
1.00
0.75
0.50
0.25
0

(Millions of 1971 Dollars)

1946   1950   1955   1960   1965   1970   1975

an annual decline of 1.9 per cent in the utilization rate, compared with a fall of 0.34 per cent in the sector. This industry group had the second highest rate of decline in capacity utilization during the 1970s.

Labour Productivity, Capital Intensity, and Real Earnings

Table 20-1 shows the average performance in the chemical industries in terms of these three variables, compared with that in total manufacturing and all other industries in the sector. Average labour productivity in the chemical and chemical products industry group was above that in the sector, and increasingly so, throughout all the periods. Relative to all other industries in the sector it was fifth in the 1950s, fourth in the 1960s, and third in the 1970s. Average capital intensity in this group increased continuously and was more than twice the sector average throughout. It was among the highest in the sector in

TABLE 20-1

AVERAGE ANNUAL PERFORMANCE OF LABOUR PRODUCTIVITY,
CAPITAL INTENSITY, AND REAL EARNINGS,
CHEMICAL AND CHEMICAL PRODUCTS INDUSTRIES

	Chemical	Total Manu.	Industry/ Sector
	(1971 $/hour)		(%)
Labour Productivity			
1946-77	6.76	4.93	137.1
1946-60	4.36	3.50	124.6
1960-70	7.34	5.34	137.5
1970-77	11.06	7.43	148.9
1973-77	11.81	7.79	151.6
Capital Intensity			
1946-77	13.33	5.58	238.9
1946-60	9.08	4.47	203.1
1960-70	14.05	6.67	210.6
1970-77	21.41	9.11	235.0
1973-77	23.37	9.53	245.2
Real Earnings			
1946-77	3.11	2.75	113.1
1946-60	2.26	2.07	109.2
1960-70	3.45	2.96	116.6
1970-77	4.35	3.79	114.8
1973-77	4.46	3.92	113.8

terms of average capital intensity, ranking third in the 1950s, fourth in the 1960s, and second in the 1970s. Average real earnings also increased from one decade to the next throughout, with the largest average increase occurring between the 1950s and the 1960s. This industry group's average earnings level fluctuated between 9 and 14 per cent above that of the sector throughout the whole period. Relative to all other industries in the sector, this group ranked, in terms of average earnings, fourth in the 1950s and 1960s and sixth during the 1970-77 period.

Table 20-2 gives the annual rate of growth of the same variables so that their progression through time could be assessed and compared with those in other industries. The compounded annual rate of labour

TABLE 20-2

COMPOUNDED ANNUAL RATES OF CHANGE IN LABOUR PRODUCTIVITY, CAPITAL INTENSITY, AND REAL EARNINGS, CHEMICAL AND CHEMICAL PRODUCTS INDUSTRIES

(% in 1971 constant dollars)

	Chemical	Total Manu.	Industry/ Sector
Labour Productivity			
1946-77	4.77	3.70	128.9
1946-60	5.59	3.82	146.3
1960-70	3.51	3.64	96.4
1970-77	4.96	3.53	140.5
1970-73	8.38	5.04	166.3
1973-77	2.46	2.41	102.1
Capital Intensity			
1946-77	5.63	3.83	147.0
1946-60	6.96	4.99	139.5
1960-70	2.29	2.34	97.9
1970-77	7.88	3.66	215.3
1970-73	3.45	1.90	181.6
1973-77	11.33	5.01	226.1
Real Earnings			
1946-77	3.35	2.85	117.5
1946-60	4.00	3.27	122.3
1960-70	3.37	2.94	114.6
1970-77	2.04	2.31	88.3
1970-73	0.32	2.72	11.8
1973-77	3.35	2.01	166.7

productivity decreased from 5.6 per cent in the 1950s to 3.5 per cent annually in the 1960s. In the 1950s it was 46 per cent above the sector's rate, whereas in the 1960s it was only 96 per cent of the sector annual rate of growth. In the 1970-77 period the annual rate of growth in labour productivity increased to 5 per cent and was 41 per cent above that of the sector. In the post-energy crisis years, the annual rates of growth of this industry group and the sector were the same. This group's labour productivity rates of growth ranked third in the 1950s and seventh in the 1960s and 1970s. When the 1970-77 period was divided into two subperiods to observe the pre- and post-energy crisis years, we found tremendous fluctuations in the rate of growth, perhaps because of an extremely large statistical error over such short periods of time. The most that could be said is that the rate of growth of labour productivity in 1973-77 seems to be far smaller than that in 1970-73.

The annual rate of growth in real earnings did not fluctuate consistently with that of labour productivity in this industry group. Table 20-2 shows that the rates of growth in real earnings were consistently lower than those of labour productivity and closer to those of the sector. Within the industry group there was a decline of 0.6 percentage points in the rate of growth between the 1950s and the 1960s, versus a 2.0 percentage point drop in the rate of growth in labour productivity. The industry group experienced a further decline of 1.3 percentage points in the growth of real earnings in the 1970-77 period, while that of labour productivity increased by 1.5 percentage points per year. In that period the industries' earnings rate of growth was 88 per cent of the sector's, while the labour productivity rate of growth in the industry outperformed that in the sector by 41 per cent (Figure 20-2).

Next we examine the severe fluctuations in the annual rates of growth in capital intensity and observe their connection to those of labour productivity (Table 20-2). The annual rate of growth of this variable declined from the 1950s to the 1960s by 4.7 percentage points, while the annual rate of decline in labour productivity was only 2.1 per cent. From the 1960s to the 1970s the annual rate of growth in capital intensity rose by 5.6 percentage points while growth rate of labour productivity increased by 1.5 percentage points. These rates of change are viewed simultaneously in Figure 20-2, where it is quite clear that from 1970 onward the rates of change in capital intensity were accelerating at a faster pace than those of labour productivity. It is, therefore, difficult to support recent claims that the main source of

FIGURE 20-2

RATES OF CHANGE IN LABOUR PRODUCTIVITY, CAPITAL INTENSITY, REAL EARNINGS, AND ECONOMIES OF SCALE, CHEMICAL AND CHEMICAL PRODUCTS INDUSTRIES (in 1971 constant dollars)

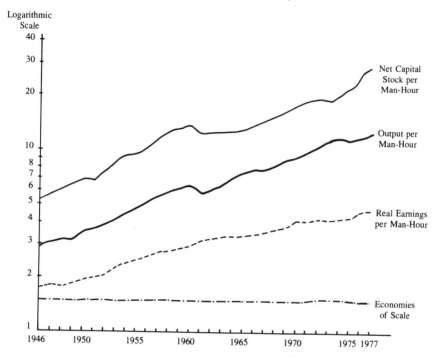

the productivity slowdown was the decline in the rate of growth in capital intensity.

Table 20-3 shows the relationship between labour productivity and real earnings, as well as computations of capital productivity in this industry. The average annual ratios of labour productivity to real earnings were above the sectoral levels throughout all the periods. Although these averages are used by some analysts, they do not carry significant economic meaning or policy implications for labour or management. More interesting is whether labour was paid its contribution to increased productivity during the various periods. In fact, in the 1950s labour received 71.4 per cent of its contribution to increased productivity. In the 1960s, however, the situation changed and labour received exactly its contribution to increased productivity.

TABLE 20-3

RATIO OF LABOUR PRODUCTIVITY/EARNINGS, OUTPUT/CAPITAL, AND TECHNOLOGICAL CHANGE, CHEMICALS AND CHEMICAL PRODUCTS INDUSTRIES

(in 1971 constant dollars)

	1946-77	1946-60	1960-70	1970-77	1970-73	1973-77
	AVERAGE LABOUR PRODUCTIVITY/AVERAGE REAL EARNINGS					
Total manufacturing	1.79	1.69	1.80	1.96		1.99
Chemical	2.17	1.93	2.13	2.54		2.65
	COMPOUNDED RATES OF CHANGE IN LABOUR PRODUCTIVITY/REAL EARNINGS					
Total manufacturing	1.30	1.17	1.24	1.53	1.85	1.20
Chemical	1.42	1.40	1.04	2.43	26.19	0.73
	AVERAGE OUTPUT/AVERAGE CAPITAL					
Total manufacturing	0.80	0.80	0.81	0.82	0.83	0.82
Chemical	0.50	0.49	0.47	0.53	0.56	0.52
	COMPOUNDED RATES OF CHANGE IN OUTPUT/CAPITAL					
Total manufacturing	−0.14	−1.14	1.30	−0.16	2.95	−2.43
Chemical	−0.81	−1.26	1.19	−2.70	7.79	−7.95
	COMPOUNDED RATES OF CHANGE IN TECHNOLOGY					
	1946-77	1960-70	1970-77			
Total manufacturing	0.271	0.259	0.361			
Chemical	−1.144	−0.106	−1.594			

In the 1970-77 period the annual rate of growth in labour productivity was more than twice the annual rate of growth in real earnings. Labour received only 41.2 per cent of its contribution to increased productivity in this industry group. It seems clear that labour was not a threat to profits in this industry or a cause for escalating prices.

So far there was no correspondence between the rates of declining productivity growth and those of capital intensity rates of growth, though the rates of growth in capital productivity are usually a source of similar behaviour in labour productivity rates of growth. Table 20-3 provides some insight into the question of capital productivity. The rate of growth in productivity of capital declined by 1.26 per cent per year during the 1950s. During that decade labour productivity increased by an annual rate of 5.6 per cent, and capital intensity by 7.0 per cent per annum. In the 1970-77 period there was an annual rate of decline of 2.7 per cent in the productivity of capital, while labour productivity increased by 5.0 per cent per annum and that of capital intensity increased by 7.9 per cent per year.

These findings do not seem to indicate the existence of a direct relationship between the productivity of capital and labour as seen in most of the other industries so far. However, they do show that in periods when capital intensity increased at a relatively high annual rate of growth, the rate of capital productivity declined. This may indicate that the industry's capacity to absorb capital while increasing its productivity was below the rate of 7.0 per cent per annum in the 1950s and 7.9 per cent per annum in the 1970s. The objective of capital intensification is to increase the productivity of labour and capital, and in this industry such an objective could have been attained with a lower rate of growth of capital intensity.

Evidence from our estimates of the VES production function shows that total productivity growth attributable to technological change in this industry was, on average, 3.5 per cent, compared with the sectoral average of 2.9 per cent over the whole period. The question then is how the industry would respond to new technology. One answer to this policy question stems from the results obtained from the m variable in the VES production function, which measures the impact of technology on labour efficiency in a form of elasticity of response. The value of m for this industry group is 2.17, which means that capital is highly complementary to labour efficiency in the production process. In terms of elasticity of response it implies that an addition of 1 per cent in technological innovation would result in an increase of 2.17 per cent in labour efficiency, the highest value in the sector.

Technological Change, Elasticity of Substitution, Labour Share, and Economies of Scale

Table 20-3 also demonstrates that the industry's technical rate of change was continuously in the direction of capital-using or labour-saving technology. Figure 20-3 gives more detail, showing that from 1946 to 1955 g declined from 1.2 to 1.0, or from slightly labour-using towards "neutral" technology. From 1957 until 1977 (with an exception of a "jump" in 1961) the industry group experienced a decline in g from 0.95 to 0.84. The elasticity of substitution variable was above one throughout the whole period, declining from a value of 4.0 in 1946 to a value of 2.0 in 1977, while the value of g declined from 1.2 in 1946 to 0.84 in 1977.

Figure 20-4 shows the pattern of change in real earnings and in the labour share of value added in this industry group. The share of labour declined from 58 per cent in 1946 to 38 per cent in 1977, and thus the share of capital increased from 42 per cent in 1946 to 62 per cent in

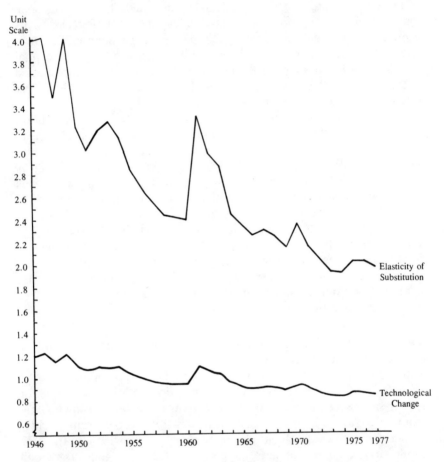

1977. The pattern of fluctuations of labour share, compared with those of real earnings per hour paid, reveals that real earnings increased at a faster rate when the share of labour showed a more significant downward trend, particularly after 1966.

The relationship between economies of scale and productivity is the final area of observation. Estimates from three different production functions showed that this industry group experienced economies of scale of 1.45 to 1.49, so that a 1 per cent increase in factor inputs

204

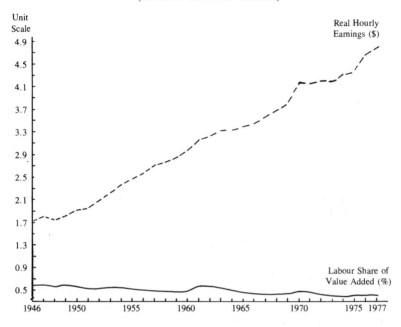

FIGURE 20-4
RATE OF EARNINGS AND LABOUR SHARE OF VALUE ADDED,
CHEMICAL AND CHEMICAL PRODUCTS INDUSTRIES
(in 1971 constant dollars)

resulted in a 1.47 per cent increase in total output. Figure 20-2 shows that economies of scale were fairly constant through time at 1.49 in 1946 and 1.48 in 1977. Estimates from the Translog production function also show that economies of scale increased, though at a decreasing but statistically insignificant rate. The Diwan test demonstrated that economies of scale accounted for 10 per cent of the growth in labour productivity. From these findings, it is difficult to establish a relationship between economies of scale and productivity in this industry group.

205

Conclusion

Several major findings emerged from the detailed analysis of the nineteen manufacturing industries of the Standard Industrial Classification. They are summarized in terms of the aggregate industry-wide results and at the level of industry groups.

- On aggregate, labour productivity in the manufacturing sector grew at a faster annual rate than capital intensity throughout the thirty-two-year period.
- Labour efficiency in the sector did not depend significantly on capital intensity; nor has capital stock proved to be highly complementary to labour.
- While the rate of growth of average capital productivity (output-capital ratio) declined, the rate of growth in the productivity of capital appeared to be almost constant in the sector as a whole.
- The technology of the sector was slightly capital saving throughout the period, with the contribution of technological change to increases in total productivity during the thirty-two-year period averaging about 2.5 per cent annually.
- The sector enjoyed a significant level of economies of scale throughout, with a relatively high level of capacity utilization.
- The relationship between increases in labour productivity and those of real hourly earnings was consistent through time. During the last three decades the rate of increase in productivity outstripped that in real earnings.
- Real average hourly earnings increased continuously throughout the period from $1.65 in 1946 to $4.06 in 1977. The share of payments to labour out of total value added gradually decreased, however, from 61 per cent in 1946 to 49 per cent in 1977.

These findings are interesting, but useful only to a limited extent because of the wide variations in industry performance in all categories of our analysis. In what follows, we summarize the industries' performance in terms of the variables in categories established in Volume I and followed at the industry level in this volume.

Capacity Utilization

By definition no industry can operate continuously at 100 per cent capacity utilization. An industry utilizing its resources optimally would stay continuously close to capacity operation, but this phenomenon has been the exception rather than the rule in the manufacturing sector throughout the thirty-two-year period.

Six industry groups, comprising 49 per cent of the sector's value added, operated well below capacity during the total period. Only four industry groups conformed with the capacity utilization pattern of the total manufacturing sector, reaching full capacity in 1973. In the different periods capacity utilization varied considerably among industries. Six industry groups operated below their potential capacity utilization since 1960. The 1965-77 period looks even worse, since thirteen industry groups, representing 71 per cent of the sector's value added, operated well below their full capacity potential. This simply means that these industries reached their capacity prior to 1965 and have not recovered since.

In the 1973-77 subperiod the rate of capacity utilization declined in all the industries in the sector. Seven industry groups experienced an annual compounded rate of decline greater than the sectoral average. The remaining twelve industry groups' rate of decline was smaller than the sector average; nevertheless, their performance diverged continuously from their potential output levels.

These rates of decline are worrisome. The sources of such a decline in capacity utilization rates vary for different industries. For a few industries weakening domestic and external demand could very well be a dominant factor. For other industries the decline could be attributed to the supply side; that is, to a declining rate of average capital productivity and declining rate of growth in the productivity of capital in the 1970-73 subperiod, partly because of the accumulation of low-productivity capital stock.

Economies of Scale

Most of the estimated economies of scale coefficients were consistent in the three production functions; that is, the absolute level of economies of scale did not change in a significant way during the whole period. Fifteen industry groups enjoyed economies of scale during the last three decades. More specifically, nine industry groups experienced economies of scale of 1.5 to 1.9; six industry groups experienced economies of scale of 1.1 to 1.4; two industry groups attained constant returns to scale; and the remaining two industries experienced diseconomies of scale.

Although there were no significant shifts in the absolute levels of the scale variable—for example, no constant return to scale industry shifted into economies of scale category—there were variations within the categories and at times a general trend in a rate of change. Seven industry groups showed an average rate of decline in economies of scale, but only three industry groups decreased their scale in a highly significant way. Six industry groups showed a statistically significant increase in their scale parameter, while the remaining eight industry groups show no change throughout the period.

From 1970 to 1973 economies of scale increased in most industries, with the variation of such an increase ranging from 0.01 to 0.49 percentage points per annum. After 1973, however, five industry groups showed a decline ranging from 0.02 to 0.38 percentage points per year. Slackening demand could account for such a decline.

Labour Productivity

Average labour productivity was below the sectoral average in six industries and above it in eight over the 1946-77 period. In the 1960-77 period, eleven industries were above the sector average, while eight industries were below it. In the 1970-77 period, ten industry groups were above the sectoral average, while nine industries were below it. In the 1973-77 subperiod there was no change.

The analysis of annual rate-of-change data provided a different picture. In the 1946-77 period the rate of change in labour productivity in ten industry groups was above the sector average, below it in seven industry groups, and equivalent to it in two industries. In the 1960-70 decade twelve industry groups experienced a slower rate of growth in productivity than the sector, while four industries had a higher rate of growth than the sector. In the 1970-77 period most industry groups experienced an accelerated rate of growth in labour productivity. Fifteen industries experienced a higher rate of growth than the sector rate, while three industries progressed at a lower rate than the sector. There was a slight change in the 1973-77 subperiod, when fourteen industries exhibited an annual rate of growth in productivity above the sector rate, while five experienced a slower rate of growth than that in the sector. Interestingly, in the 1970-73 subperiod there was a decrease in the rate of growth in the productivity of labour in all nineteen industry groups, while in the 1973-77 subperiod we saw a complete reversal: an increase in the rate of growth in the productivity of labour in all nineteen industries.

The contribution of economies of scale to labour productivity growth ranged widely, from a contribution of up to 10 per cent in five industry groups, between 23 to 31 per cent in seven industries, and to nothing in seven industry groups. Calculating the impact of technology on labour efficiency showed that seven industry groups were highly responsive to the introduction of new technology—that is, capital was highly complementary to an increase in labour efficiency—six industry groups had an average response, while six industry groups showed no or a very slight response to the introduction of new technology.

Capital Intensity

Generally, capital intensity increased in the manufacturing sector after 1946. In the 1946-60 period the rate of growth in capital intensity exceeded the average rate of growth in the total period (1946-77). In the 1960-70 decade, however, the rate of growth declined in seventeen out of the nineteen industry groups. The trend changed in the 1970-77 period: only three industries retained the rates of growth of the 1960s, five industries showed a decline in their rates of growth, while eleven industry groups experienced an increase in the rate of capital intensification. But in the 1973-77 subperiod, seventeen industries accelerated their annual rate of growth in capital intensity.

In the 1946-77 period the rate of growth in capital intensity was greater than that of labour productivity in nine industry groups. In only four industry groups had the rate of growth of capital intensity outstripped that of labour productivity in all periods. During the 1946-60 period ten industries experienced a greater rate of growth of capital intensity than labour productivity.

In the 1960-70 decade the rate of growth in labour productivity was greater than that of capital intensity in fourteen industries. An acceleration in the rate of capital intensity in the 1970-77 period was evident, when in eleven industry groups the annual rate of growth of capital intensity was considerably greater than that of labour productivity. In the 1973-77 subperiod that set of eleven industries expanded to fifteen out of the sector's nineteen industries.

Technological Progress

The average impact of technology on total productivity during the whole period was statistically significant and above the sectoral average only in seven industry groups of the sector. In six industry groups technological progress did not have any significant impact on productivity. An investigation of the type of technology used by the industries during the three decades revealed that eleven industry groups employed capital-using technology, three industries employed labour-using technology, and the technology was neutral in five industries.

The rate of change analysis showed that in the 1946-77 period six industry groups progressed in the direction of capital-using technology; eight industry groups experienced a continuous change towards labour-using technology. In the 1960s, six industry groups utilized labour-saving technology, eleven progressed through labour-using technology, while two industries show no change. In the 1970-77 period, ten industry groups experienced a change towards capital-using technology, seven industries became more labour-intensive, and in two industries there was no change. It may be interesting to note that only six of the twelve highly capital-intensive industries showed significant effect on rates of change in technology of production.

Elasticity of Substitution

This measure is of the biased type computed from the VES production function and shows the ease with which labour could be substituted by capital without altering total output. The findings show that in eleven industries of the sector such substitution is not feasible. These industries represent most of the sector's value added output. Such substitution is feasible in six industries and neutral in two industry groups. These findings imply that the sector could provide employment opportunities only by its absolute expansion, because technical change from capital intensiveness to labour intensiveness would jeopardise productivity.

Real Earnings and Labour Share

Real earnings per hour paid increased in all the sector's industries in the 1946-77 period. I did not, however, find a consistent pattern in the rate of growth of real earnings across the industries through time. Total manufacturing showed a decreasing trend in the annual rate of growth of real earnings per hour. Only four industries followed such a trend. Five industry groups showed an increasing trend in the earnings rate of change, while the remaining ten industry groups showed no consistent upward or downward trend. Total payments to labour as a share in value added increased only in three industry groups. The share of labour decreased in sixteen industry groups during the 1946-77 period.

210

A comparison of average earnings per hour and their rates of growth with average labour productivity (output per hour) and its rates of growth in different periods revealed some interesting insights. Average hourly real earnings were lower than average labour productivity in all industries and in all subperiods. When rates of growth were computed, I found that in the 1946-77 period the annual rate of growth in real earnings exceeded that in labour productivity only in two industry groups. In three industry groups the two rates of growth were similar, while in fourteen industry groups the rate of increase in productivity outstripped that of real earnings. In the 1960-70 period, the rate of growth in real earnings was greater than that of productivity in nine industry groups. In ten industries, however, the rate of growth in productivity exceeded that of real earnings. The pattern of the early 1970s signifies an improvement over the 1960s.

During 1970-77 the rate of growth of productivity exceeded the rate of growth in real earnings in thirteen industry groups. In five industries, however, the rate of growth in real earnings was higher than that of productivity. In the post-energy crisis subperiod, there was an acceleration in the rate of growth of real earnings in seven industries. In these seven industry groups the rate of growth in earnings was greater than that of productivity by a factor of 1.3 to 5.3. In twelve industry groups the rate of growth in productivity continued to outstrip that in real earnings.

The Main Findings

In sum, the main findings of this analysis are as follows. First, there is no strict correspondence between economies of scale and productivity, or between capital intensity and productivity. Second, the impact of technology on labour efficiency and productivity was not significant in the majority of the industries. Third, this is reflected in the diminishing contribution of capital to productivity, especially in the post-energy crisis period when the rate of change in the productivity of capital declined in eight industry groups, remained constant in five industries, and increased in only four industry groups. Fourth, the rate of change in the productivity of labour declined in the 1970-73 subperiod in eight industry groups, increased in four groups, and remained roughly the same in seven industries. In the 1973-77 subperiod, however, rate of change in the productivity of labour increased in eleven industries, decreased in six industries, and remained unchanged in two. When the 1970-77 period is analysed and compared with the 1960-70 decade, an increase in rate of change in the productivity of labour is shown in

211

seventeen out of the nineteen industries in the sector. Thus the problem of low capital productivity seems more severe than that of low labour productivity in most industries.

The Canadian Institute for Economic Policy Series

The Monetarist Counter-Revolution: A Critique of Canadian Monetary Policy 1975-1979
Arthur W. Donner and Douglas D. Peters

Canada's Crippled Dollar: An Analysis of International Trade and Our Troubled Balance of Payments ·
H. Lukin Robinson

Unemployment and Inflation: The Canadian Experience
Clarence L. Barber and John C.P. McCallum

How Ottawa Decides: Planning and Industrial Policy-Making 1968-1980
Richard D. French

Energy and Industry: The Potential of Energy Development Projects for Canadian Industry in the Eighties
Barry Beale

The Energy Squeeze: Canadian Policies for Survival
Bruce F. Willson

The Post-Keynesian Debate: A Review of Three Recent Canadian Contributions
Myron J. Gordon

Water: The Emerging Crisis in Canada
Harold D. Foster and W.R. Derrick Sewell

The Working Poor: Wage Earners and the Failure of Income Security Policies
David P. Ross

Beyond the Monetarists: Post-Keynesian Alternatives to Rampant Inflation, Low Growth and High Unemployment
Edited by David Crane

The Splintered Market: Barriers to Interprovincial Trade in Canadian Agriculture
R.E. Haack, D.R. Hughes and R.G. Shapiro

The Drug Industry: A Case Study of the Effects of Foreign Control on the Canadian Economy
Myron J. Gordon and David J. Fowler

The New Protectionism: Non-Tariff Barriers and Their Effects on Canada
Fred Lazar

Industrial Development and the Atlantic Fishery: Opportunities for Manufacturing and Skilled Workers in the 1980s
Donald J. Patton

Canada's Population Outlook: Demographic Futures and Economic Challenges
David K. Foot

Financing the Future: Canada's Capital Markets in the Eighties
Arthur W. Donner

Controlling Inflation: Learning from Experience in Canada, Europe and Japan
Clarence L. Barber and John C.P. McCallum

Canada and the Reagan Challenge: Crisis in the Canadian-American Relationship
Stephen Clarkson

The Future of Canada's Auto Industry: The Big Three and the Japanese Challenge
Ross Perry

The above titles are available from:

James Lorimer & Company, Publishers
Egerton Ryerson Memorial Building
35 Britain Street
Toronto, Ontario M5A 1R7